ALL NEW
SQUARE
FOOT
GARDENING

Published by Cool Springs Press, 500 Wilson Pike Circle, Suite 100
Brentwood, Tennessee 37027

First Printing Revised Edition 2006

Printed in the United States of America
10 9 8 7 6 5 4 3 2 1

Managing Editors: The Staff of Cool Springs Press
Designer: Bruce Gore, Gore Studios
Copyeditor: Cindy Kershner
Photography: J. Paul Moore, except for pages 37, 81, and 117.
These photos are by Neil Soderstrom.
Illustration: James Lindquist
Production Design: Marc Pewitt

Visit the Cool Springs Press website at **www.coolspringspress.net**.

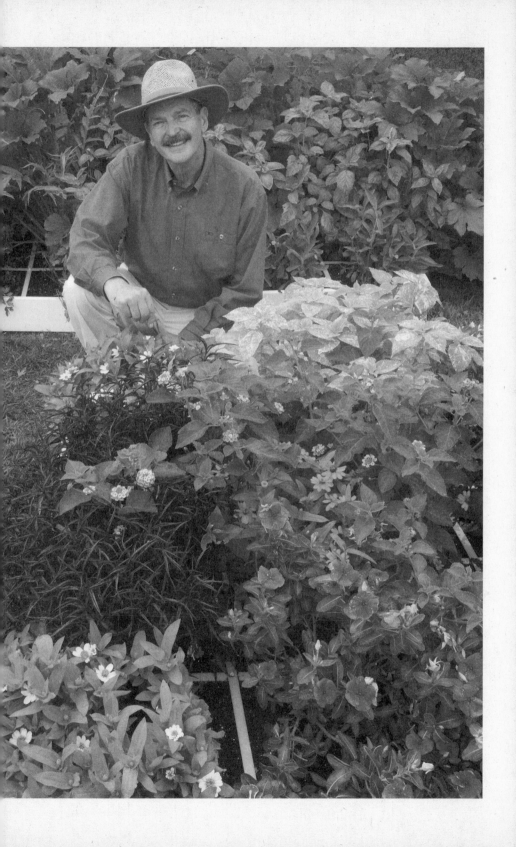

Dedication

This book is dedicated to the loving memory of my daughter, Gail Bartholomew (1954–2000). Gail was my biggest supporter and was one of the original members of the Board of Directors for the Square Foot Gardening Foundation. She was most enthusiastic about our school gardening program.

Acknowledgments

I am most fortunate to be surrounded by a dedicated staff who not only worked many late nights getting this book ready, but who truly believe in and are dedicated to the principles of Square Foot Gardening.

Brenda Grow
Typist

Lori Pelkowski
Researcher

and Karen Bastow
My most able and devoted assistant

• • •

MEL BARTHOLOMEW

COOL
SPRINGS
PRESS

Growing Successful Gardeners™
www.coolspringspress.net
FRANKLIN, TENNESSEE

Contents

Introduction

Why write an updated version of the best selling gardening book of all time? The old saying goes, "If it ain't broke, don't fix it." Well, Square Foot Garden isn't broken, but the **all new** model is so superior, so much simpler, and so improved that you can now forget all about the original book and the original Square Foot Gardening method!

What's so new about the All New Square Foot Gardening book? The original can be considered the Model T of Square Foot Gardening. This new one . . . like the latest Cadillac! They are both cars and they both move down the road . . . but—oh boy—what a difference!

In this expanded and revised book on Square Foot Gardening, you too can learn, as millions of others already have, how to become a successful gardener the simple and painless way. This easy-to-understand method will revolutionize the way you think about gardening; and the new ideas found in this revised edition will awe and inspire you as I share insights on how the Square Foot Gardening method can, and is, changing the world.

For Experts Only

A reporter once asked me if I thought I had invented "gardening for dummies," referring, of course, to the popular Square Foot Gardening method I developed in 1976. "No," I answered.

Actually, when I invented the Square Foot Gardening (SFG) method, I thought it would be for expert gardeners. My method was very precise and detailed, yet very simple and easy to understand, and it provided all the conditions necessary for successfully growing a broad variety of plants in a very different way. It also eliminated all of the wasteful, inefficient practices of traditional single-row gardening. I thought the experts would shout "Eureka!" and immediately bless all of the new ideas and advantages of this new home gardening method.

Beginners Understood

As it turned out, the experts never understood this unique method. Apparently it was too simple and easy. But the beginning gardener, and those discouraged by previous failed attempts, understood it completely. They immediately saw the simplicity of SFG. The beginner's instant response was "I can do this!" while the experts continued to question every aspect of this revolutionary gardening method. They just couldn't admit that home gardening could be that easy.

Two Hours or Two Weeks

In my lectures, I like to reassure audiences that if they are new at gardening, or perhaps afraid or overwhelmed by the idea of starting a garden, they will be able to learn this simple method of gardening in just an hour or two. However, if they are already "expert" gardeners, it will probably take them about two weeks! After the laughter dies down, I remind my audience that beginners readily accept the minimal amount of technical information needed to become successful gardeners because they want to know how to successfully garden.

The "experts," on the other hand, are so entrenched with the idea of single-row gardening as used in farming, with all of its wasteful methods, that they just can't see it any other way. You might say, "They are stuck in a rut." As a result, I've learned to leave the experts alone and concentrate on the beginner, or the tried-but-failed, gardener, and even the afraid-to-start person.

SFG appeals to other large groups of would-be gardeners. Years ago, I read some very interesting statistics (and I'm sure the percentages are similar today) about these gardeners.

75 Million vs. 10 Million

Every year there are about 15 million people who:

- would like to begin gardening.
- tried the traditional single-row gardening method, but failed.
- don't want to begin gardening because they have heard of all the hard work, time, and cost associated with gardening.
- are doing single-row gardening but are tired of the hard work, time, and cost associated with this impractical method.
- are unable to continue caring for their big single-row gardens.

Combined, that's an estimated **75 million** people ready for a gardening revolution compared to about **10 million** single-row gardeners who are content with their method and don't want to change.

Twenty-Five Years and One Million Books Later

The first book I wrote on SFG in 1981 lasted twenty-five years and sold over one million copies, becoming the best selling gardening book in America. Here is the story behind how I came to invent a better way to garden, and the ultimate success of SFG.

It Started in 1975

It all started in 1975 after my retirement from my consulting engineering business in New Jersey. In celebration, I moved my family to a waterfront home on the North Shore of Long Island. After a year of rebuilding the house and another year of landscaping and improving the grounds, I decided to take up gardening as a hobby. My first step was to attend a lecture on composting given by a local environmental group. It was a warm spring day in April—a great time to be out in the garden. A small group milled around at the advertised meeting point, but no instructor ever showed up. So, rather than disband, I suggested to the group that we each share our knowledge with each other and tell what little we knew about composting. We had a wonderful time and actually learned a little bit from each other. As we prepared to leave, someone asked me, "Can we do this again next week?" And I said, "Sure, why not?" Thus began my new career of teaching gardening while I was still a novice myself.

Community Garden

The next step was organizing a community garden for this same environmental group. I found some land and convinced the town to cut down all the weeds and fence it in. A local farmer delivered two truckloads of well-rotted manure, and, after the ground was all fertilized and plowed up, we laid out plots and aisles and opened for business. All of the spaces were quickly taken by people in the community, and everyone started with great enthusiasm. Since most of the participants didn't have a garden at home and were novices, they were enthusiastic about obtaining instruction and insights on gardening.

So I initiated a Saturday morning gardening workshop and presented information on a different subject each week while everyone sat around on bales of hay listening. I was teaching basic single-row gardening because that's all anyone knew back then. I was busy studying and learning gardening myself, trying to keep ahead of everyone's questions! The local county agricultural agent helped out and everything went well until about midsummer. It was about then that our once-enthusiastic gardeners stopped coming out to the garden. However, the weeds kept coming—and growing! Pretty soon the place was overgrown and looked a mess.

First Red Flag

I was discouraged and thought I had better do some research to figure out why we had failed, so I visited many backyard gardens.

What I found was a big space way out in the farthest corner of the yard, about as close to the neighbor's property line as possible. In most cases, these individual gardens were also filled with overgrown weeds. The first red flag went up in my mind, indicating that there was something wrong with traditional single-row gardening. I began to think about all the conventional gardening practices we'd been taught and began to question the efficiency of each.

Three-Foot Aisles

I questioned why fertilizer is spread over the entire garden area, but the plants are only placed in long, skinny rows with 3-foot wide aisles on both sides. I wondered why you were supposed to till up all the soil in an entire garden area when those 3-foot wide aisles consume over 80 percent of a garden area, although plants in rows require less than 20 percent of the garden space. Then I wondered why you would walk all over the rest of the garden area again, packing down all that newly tilled soil? And, why is an entire garden area watered when plants are only located in a 6-inch wide row in the center of a 6-foot wide strip?

Too Many, Too Much

As I analyzed these traditional gardening methods, I realized that there is only one outcome you can expect when you fertilize and water a 3-foot wide aisle with nothing planted in it—**weeds**!

The following is a conversation I had with a friend of mine who was an agricultural agent.

"Why a 3-foot wide aisle on both sides of the planted row?" I asked.

Mel Bartholomew

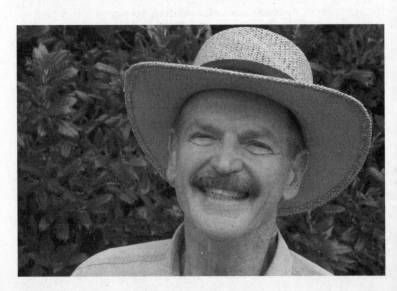

"So you have room to get into the garden to hoe the weeds," he replied.

"But I don't want to hoe the weeds," I protested. "That's too much work."

"Well," he said, "let's face it. Gardening is a lot of hard work."

This triggered another red flag in my mind. Gardening shouldn't be a lot of hard work. Gardening should be fun! There's something wrong here.

This led to further questions. Why do the planting instructions on packages of seeds direct the gardener to pour out an entire packet along a row only to have you later go back and tear out 95 percent of the seeds you planted once they sprout? Why use up an entire $1.89 packet of seeds for every row you plant? Isn't that rather wasteful? Why would they instruct us to plant that way? Who's in charge here, anyway?

Thirty-Foot Rows

The next question I asked was why plant an entire row of everything? Just because my garden is 30 feet long, for example, do I really want or need a whole row of cabbages? That would be thirty cabbages spaced 12 inches apart. This brings me to another commonsense revelation that no one seems to have thought about. Why would I want thirty cabbages to ripen all at the same time? If everything is planted at one time, won't it also be ready to harvest all at once? It sounds like farming to me, but that's too much to enjoy at the same time for a homeowner. How many people go to the grocery store and buy thirty heads of cabbage once a year? Do you? So why grow it that way? There must be a better way to stagger the harvest, and the obvious solution is to stagger the time of planting whenever possible and to plant less.

Because That's the Way

I soon realized that I had a lot of questions with very few answers, so I traveled all over the country seeking out the best experts: agricultural college professors, county agricultural agents, garden writers, radio and TV gardening personalities, gardening publishers, book writers, garden clubs—all those who were supposedly knowledgeable people in the field of gardening. I sought answers to all the gardening questions I had and, no matter where I traveled throughout the country from Maine to California, I kept receiving the same answer. Can you imagine what that answer was? It soon became apparent that the only reason traditional single-row gardening methods continued to exist was, **"Because that's the way we've always done it!"** Right then and there I said, "I'm going to invent a better way to garden."

Farming

Part of the problem, I realized, was that single-row gardening was nothing but a hand-me-down technique from large-field crop farming. Single rows make sense when you depend upon a mule or a tractor to plow up the soil and tend the crops because those big hooves or wheels take up a lot of room. But why had no one ever realized that in a home garden, there is no longer a need for all that wasted space. There only needs to be room for two feet—yours! Yet, every single direction for home gardening still instructs, "Space rows 3 feet apart." Perhaps **that's** really the gardening method for dummies!

Efficiency

The next step I took was to list all of the ineffective, inefficient, and unnecessary steps that have been consistently taught for traditional single-row gardening and then find a better and more efficient way to accomplish the same task. I should mention here that besides being a civil engineer, I was also an efficiency expert. Before I sold my engineering company, my job was to travel to construction sites or manufacturing facilities to analyze current processes in order to identify and correct inefficiencies in facility operations. In other words, to find a better way. Thus, the challenge of inventing a new way to garden was right up my alley. The sequence of questions I asked and simple solutions I developed was actually very easy and straightforward, but it involved a little out-of-the-box thinking. Follow me along now.

One Thousand Seeds

I have fun when teaching a class or seminar by asking, "How many seeds do you think are in a packet of leaf lettuce?" Some guess fifty, one hundred, two hundred, and some even venture a guess as high as five hundred seeds. I then astound them by saying that I once opened a packet and counted them, and there were well over one thousand seeds! Why plant hundreds of seeds in one long row, and then turn around when they sprout and thin them out to one plant for every 6 inches? It doesn't make sense, does it? It's a terrible waste of seeds and time and work—all useless, unnecessary work. My first solution was to lay down a yardstick and plant one seed every 6 inches. Then, I had nothing further to do and no wasted seeds. The next thought was, if you're growing, for example, lettuce, and the seed packet says to thin plants to 6 inches apart in the row, how far away does the next row really need to be? The answer, of course, is 6 inches—not 3 feet!

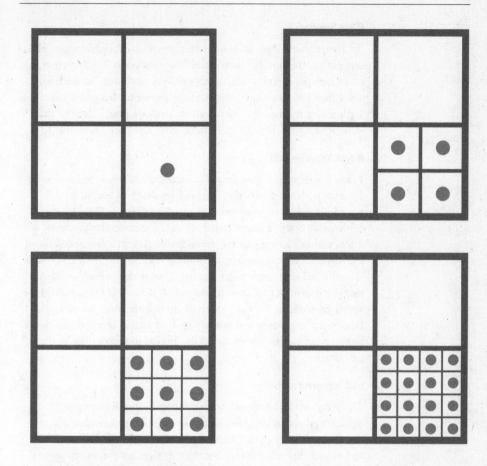

Single Row, Double Row, Triple Row

Eager to test my reasoning, I planted two rows, 6 inches apart, to see how well the plants would do. It worked! The plants grew just as well in two rows as they did in a single row, as long as each plant had 6 inches all around. Next I tried a triple row—three rows where I placed all the plants 6 inches apart in all directions. Again, it worked! How wide could I make this, I asked? The answer is, as wide as you can reach in to maintain your garden; in other words, as long as your arms. But I still had a harvest too large to utilize.

Depending on the mature size of each plant, space a couple of seeds or transplants one, four, nine, or sixteen per square foot.

Shorten the Rows

So what was the obvious solution? Shorten the rows! And they kept getting shorter and shorter, until they were only 12 inches long and 12 inches wide—a square foot planting area. How many plants could you grow in that square foot if each plant was 6 inches apart? The simple answer: four plants per square foot.

Plant Spacing

So, in summary, if plants should be thinned to 12 inches apart, plant one per square foot. If plants should be thinned to 6 inches apart, plant four per square foot. If plants should be thinned to 4 inches apart then you can grow nine within the space of that one square foot. If plants are thinned to 3 inches apart, you can grow sixteen in that same square foot. Doesn't it all make sense and seem easy enough?

Never Walk on Soil

I then wondered just how far someone could reach in to maintain a garden without compacting the soil by walking all over it. So, I got a little old lady and a big husky man and measured how far they could easily reach. I found that both could comfortably reach in 2 feet without losing balance. In order to reach in 2 feet and walk all the way around your garden, you end up having a 4×4-foot area. Now, the only soil that needs to be dug up, improved, watered, and fertilized is a 4×4-foot garden area and not all the aisles. That reduced the actual growing area in the garden by 80 percent. And, an added benefit is the growing soil in the 4×4-foot area is never packed down, so you don't have to hoe or dig up the ground to keep loosening the planting soil.

Soil Improvement

The next step was how to improve the soil. After listening to agricultural agents and reading books on soil improvement and conditioning, the only option seemed to require a great deal of work, time, and money. My research indicated that average soil conditions around the country were not well-suited for growing healthy vegetables and beautiful flowers. Thus, in most areas soils had to be greatly improved to obtain the best gardening results.

Horse Manure

Most soils only contain about 3 or 4 percent organic material. Thus, the traditional first step for improving soil in preparation for gardening was to dig or till up the soil in the entire garden as deep as you could and then add soil enhancers such as compost or well-rotted manure followed later by commercial fertilizers. This initial step rang a bell with me because, as a teenager, I was the one who had to turn over my mother's garden, digging the whole thing up every year. My father had to bring home bushel baskets full of horse manure in his brand new Chrysler. After we dumped it into the garden area, I had to do all of the spreading, mixing, and turning. As laborers in Mom's garden every spring, my dad and I were not happy campers, although she was thrilled with the results.

The Seven-Year Itch

I once conducted a survey, asking gardeners how long it took them to improve their soil until they got it just the way they wanted it. The average answer was about seven years—seven years of hard work to properly condition the soil for gardening! And do you know what statistics say the average homeowner does after seven years? They move! And guess who buys that home? Someone who doesn't even garden!

You can probably imagine the conversation between the new homeowners. "Henry, let's pave over that garden area; it would make a great place to park the trailer." Seven years worth of effort lost. There's something definitely wrong with this scenario.

Start Right in a Single Day

I started thinking, "Why not have great soil during the first year of your garden, and every year thereafter, no matter where you live?" Of course, with traditional big garden areas, having the best soil conditions right away may be too costly and entail too much time and effort. Remember that after I did the math, I found that by switching from a traditional single-row garden to a 4×4-foot layout —which will produce the same harvest—80 percent of the garden area could be completely eliminated. This means that you can grow 100 percent of the harvest in only 20 percent of the space. That 80 percent of a single-row garden is wasted space—space that doesn't need to be fertilized, watered, or improved, but it does have to be weeded. Think of it. With the SFG method, seven years worth of work can suddenly be condensed into as little as a single day without all the effort!

The 4x4-Foot Garden

My first book showed how you could reduce the work by laying out a 4×4-foot area, then digging out 6 inches of existing soil and mixing in 2 inches of peat moss, 2 inches of vermiculite, and 2 inches of compost. These ingredients are available at any nursery. Many gardeners even make their own compost at home from kitchen scraps and other plant material. Mixing the ingredients together with the soil that you removed, you now have 12 inches of 50 percent improved soil. My thinking was that 12 inches of improved existing soil would be all that new plants would need to thrive with the plant roots staying within these 12 inches of improved soil. But the experts I consulted said that most vegetable plant roots need to keep growing downward, searching for water and nutrients many, many feet below the surface of the soil. "But," I thought, "if plants are provided a good growing soil composed of more than 15 percent organic matter, and if vermiculite and peat moss are mixed in, helping to retain water in the soil, plant roots would no longer need to continue growing downward in search of additional moisture and nutrients." Besides that, I wondered if they were right about the roots needing to grow deeper than 12 inches, how come most rototillers dig down less than 6 inches? Well, it turned out they were wrong. Our gardens thrived with less than 12 inches of improved soil and that was just the beginning! Wait until you read Chapter 2, which describes the latest advances in this "out of the box" type of thinking.

Stagger the Harvest

I also realized that if each square foot could be planted with a different crop containing either one, four, nine, or sixteen plants, all properly spaced, it wouldn't be necessary to plant a whole row of just one crop. So, why not stagger your vegetable plantings, so that your harvest is also staggered? Makes sense, doesn't it? Yet we've been taught all our lives to plant everything all at once in long rows—another hand-me-down technique from large-field crop farming. If you're farming for commercial purposes, you want everything to ripen at once so it can be harvested together and taken to market. But with home gardening, you want to stagger your produce so you can use it throughout the season for daily consumption.

Of course, I'm not talking about canning, freezing, and other home-storage measures, although SFG is a practical gardening method for these purposes also. However, I've found that people are not storing homegrown produce to the extent they did in the past. Remember, I grew up in the days of the "victory garden," a result of World War II when Americans were encouraged by the government and by society to have a big garden that used the old single-row planting methods. Most people who grew up during those years hated gardening because of all the weeding and hard work it entailed. That carried over into a whole generation of people who stayed away from gardening just because of the negative memories associated with maintaining a large traditional garden. And, I might add, also from all the work of canning and freezing. So why does the government still teach the same old system more than 60 years later?

Stop Planting So Much

I meet many mature couples where the husband proudly states, "I have a big single-row garden, and I grow a lot of produce." And the woman responds, "Oh, but I wish he'd stop. He grows all this produce that we really don't need anymore. Then I have to can and freeze it. I'm tired and don't want to do it anymore. We don't need it but he just keeps growing it!" With SFG, you don't have to grow so much at a time that it becomes overwhelming.

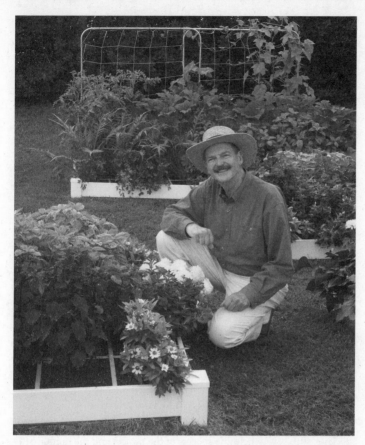

Believe me, there are so many advantages to the SFG method, and the benefits and efficiencies only continue to increase.

Location

I began to realize another great advantage of SFG—by reducing the garden size by 80 percent, it increases the number of places where a garden will fit. A garden no longer has to be way out back, snugly put up against your neighbor's property line. And since you don't have to fertilize, water, and weed the aisles, it can now be located near the house.

Up Close and Personal

"Closer is better" is one SFG motto. When a garden is closer to the front or back door of your home, you pass by the garden more often. This means it is easier to take care of and can be more readily enjoyed, all of which results in a better garden and a happier gardener. The whole package fits together nicely. There are so many advantages to Square Foot Gardening, and the benefits and efficiencies of the concept only continue to increase.

The Square Foot Gardening Story

Community Garden

Well, we tried all these new ideas in the community garden the next
year, and, guess what? They worked! Everyone understood and
grasped the Square Foot Gardening concepts quickly and easily, and
since most of the participants were beginning gardeners who were
well acquainted with the disastrous experience from the previous
year—including the overgrown weeds and mounds of zucchini and
rows of cabbage that ripened all at once—they were very willing to
try another option. That next year, 1976, we were able to enjoy a
very attractive and well-run community garden using the newly developed Square Foot method. The Bicentennial year of 1976 was
a huge celebration across the country and we also celebrated my
youngest son's July Fourth birthday. I decided to do three things: one
for my country, one for my family, and one for myself. The official
presentation of Square Foot Gardening was made at a hometown
event that included a school project that I had organized. All the
schools grew sunflowers, which were planted along Main Street as a
beautification project. We had an all-day celebration of displays,
talks, booths, and demonstrations on the new Square Foot Gardening
method I had developed. I announced this was my gift to the country—a better way to garden.

Sharing Ideas, 1978 to 1980

Because of the overwhelming success of the project and the unique SFG
method, many people encouraged me to write a book sharing my ideas.

*"You have
forever changed
gardening
for me."*
—Kanas from California

First, the local newspaper asked me to write a garden column. Then I
began writing and producing pamphlets. Soon, magazine representatives started coming out to photograph my home garden and to write
stories about my new ideas and the SFG method. The media attention
grew and grew, so I thought, "Why not write a book?" I drafted an out-
line and sent it to two publishers, which both accepted the "how to"
book on successful gardening using the new SFG method.

Garden Consulting, 1981 to 1984

At the same time, I also began doing gardening consulting work for several companies. You can imagine how "retired" I was now. One was a
fence company, and, using their products, I began to develop vertical
gardening methods, originally for tomatoes but later for all vine crops.
Another company wanted to start a gardening tool catalog. So my job
was to search the world for unique and unusual tools, test and evaluate
them, make recommendations, and then

arrange the writing of sample descriptions for the catalog. During this time, I wondered why we needed so much stuff just to garden. And, as you'll learn, I discovered that you don't.

PBS One Minute, 1981 to 1986

My publisher's predictions for my book were very modest, so they didn't promote my book the way I had hoped or even send me out for talks and appearances. Fortunately, some of the companies I was consulting for did send me on tours and allowed me to show the book and talk about Square Foot Gardening if I also explained and demonstrated their products. This proved to be a very valuable and rewarding period, and it wasn't long before a local PBS television station asked if they could send their camera crew out to my garden to shoot "A Minute in Mel's Garden" segment for the evening news. I was delighted to have the opportunity to share the SFG method. The response to that short segment was explosive. The television station received so much mail and so many telephone calls that they wanted to tape a show for broadcast every week night. So, once a week they came to my garden and taped five different segments. That again proved so popular that later they asked if I would be interested in a thirty-minute national show. You bet I was!

Thirty-Minute PBS TV Series, 1982 to 1986

To make a long story short, my show aired the following year on PBS and was picked up by enough stations along the East Coast to pay for itself. The following year I started my own production company and distributed the thirty-minute Square Foot Gardening show throughout the entire PBS system. Within three years it was picked up by every PBS station in the country and received the highest rating of any garden show. This involved a lot of travel, but it was all very exciting. My oldest son, Steve, became the show director, and we traveled around the country to different viewers' gardens that were particularly worthy of sharing with our audience. We were also invited to Disney World to shoot during the winter, an opportunity we couldn't pass up. All of this excitement and activity made it a very rewarding and exciting period of my life.

More Television Opportunities

In addition to all the above activity and travel, many other opportunities occurred with TV networks like CNN out of Atlanta, Georgia, CBN in Virginia Beach, Virginia, and several appearances on ABC, Good Morning Boston, Good Morning Philly, and many other TV spots all around the country. All of that brought in a ton of mail (whoever had heard of e-mail back then?) and activities with companies interested in developing SFG products including some big companies

such as Rubbermaid. This was exciting and eventful, yet at times stress-
ful and exhausting. Through all of it, my wife Ginny courageously
took care of everything at home and even put up with—yet never quite
got used to—the film crews coming once a week to film the PBS TV
show. It was bad enough to have the constant activity outside in the
garden, but they even invaded her kitchen to do the cooking segment. Since such a big part of gardening is in the harvest and food
preparation, I convinced PBS to let us have the first cooking segment
on a garden show. Now, of course, they all do that.

TV Book Tag

I originally offered the program to PBS free of charge if they would
give me a one-minute book tag at the end of each show. At that time,
PBS was commercial-free and had no corporate sponsors. But they
were finally convinced that it would be worthwhile, allowing me to be
the first person to have a book tag on a PBS show. As a result, a
tremendous number of orders for the SFG book were received. We
had to set up a toll-free number and a fulfillment company to process
these orders. After six years, the operation became fairly routine and
the challenge of creating something new was over. At the same time,
some PBS stations started talking like they should share in the profits
of the book sales, yet they still wanted the show free. Rather than
compromise the initial agreement, I decided to take the show off the
air and retire for the second time. This time, my retirement was
"for sure."

Discovery Network 1989 to 1991

A few years later, an agent came to me and said that he could get
the TV show back on the air. I didn't want anything to do with it;
I was happily retired. But when he offered to do all the work and
take care of all the details, I thought, "Well, what harm could there be?"
(We never learn, do we?) I finally agreed, and he sold the show to the
Discovery Network where it ran for two years and then on The
Learning Channel for another year. I again took the show off the air.
I decided that that was it—I really was retiring for good!
(Yeah, sure!)

California Schools, 1996

Five years later, when I was traveling in northern California, someone
invited me to come see a school garden. "It's a Square Foot Garden,"
they explained. I went and thought it was so impressive. The children
were really enjoying the gardening experience, and the teachers loved
it so much that I began to think that perhaps I really shouldn't be retired—I should be out teaching SFG to school children. So, again,

One of the truly great features of SFG is how easy it is for children (of all ages!) to participate.

I came out of retirement (you know the saying "fools rush in") and established a nonprofit foundation to design a program for teachers explaining how to teach Square Foot Gardening to students. The foundation also built and distributed numerous gardens throughout the country. We called the program "A Square Yard in the School Yard" since the children's gardens are sized at 3×3 feet.

Utah Schools, 1998

This phase of my life also involved a lot of travel. As I developed new staff members, we went from school to school donating gardens all the way from Maine to Florida and on to the California coast. When offering Square Foot Gardening to schools in Utah, we tried something new. Rather than going from teacher to teacher and school to school, we went straight to the state board of education. They liked our idea so much that they said, "We'll take a garden for every single grammar school in the state of Utah." We gulped and said, "Well, let's see what we can do."

Thanksgiving Point, 1999 to 2001

Over the next two years, we were able to do just that. Next, the school board asked if I would write a lesson plan for Utah teachers and students. I did, and it has now been modified for home schooling as well. We were then invited to put up a public display Square Foot Garden at Thanksgiving Point near Salt Lake City. Thousands visited the garden and, since Salt Lake City is home to the Church of Jesus Christ of Latter-day Saints (the LDS church or Mormons), SFG gained the attention of many LDS church leaders. They invited the foundation to teach SFG at the LDS Missionary.

Training Center in Provo, Utah. We showed missionaries how to instruct people living in Third World countries to become more self-sufficient by growing their own food using the Square **Meter** Gardening method, which we had converted from the Square **Foot** Gardening method.

Square Meter Gardening: SFG Humanitarian Efforts Go Global, 2001 to 2002

Opportunities for the SFG foundation just kept on growing as we became involved with additional humanitarian organizations that sent aid overseas, many of which began including the Square Meter Gardening system in their programs. SMG was designed to appeal to families in Third World countries and improve nutrition by adding fresh vegetables to their diets. It is something that can be readily done, as the soil that is used in this program is pure compost since peat moss and vermiculite is either unavailable or too expensive to obtain overseas. An added advantage is that making compost cleans up the environment and gets all the family members involved.

SFG International Training Center in Homestead, Florida

Since gardening in Utah is at a standstill all winter, the logical direction to go that time of year is south. Through our work with several international organizations headquartered in Washington, D.C., the opportunity came to spend the winter in southern Florida where we set up an SFG International Training Center in Homestead. This proved very educational for us because the weather, plants, and techniques were much more like Central and South America. We provided a three-day training seminar for the people heading to those countries as representatives of various humanitarian organizations. This enabled Square Meter Gardening to be taken to quite a variety of people and places.

Overseas

When working with people overseas, the first step is to teach them composting. Since most Third-World countries are located in tropical regions of the world, it's very easy to find materials that can be used to generate compost. One of the biggest successes in Square Meter Gardening is a project developed in India. It illustrates how easy it is to offer meaningful foreign aid to countries without spending millions of dollars. It is also a successful way of encouraging independence rather than dependence on governmental bureaucracies. This success story began after a priest named Father Abraham received the Square Foot Gardening book. He read it and said, "We can do this!" As a result, he now operates a sizeable, well-organized 6-acre training center where hundreds—perhaps thousands— of people have come to learn the Square Meter Gardening method. The people are learning to successfully grow crops they can not only use at home but can take to market where they earn twenty times more than they did previously growing crops the traditional single-row way.

Single Rows Throughout the World

Believe it or not, many people around the world still garden and grow crops in single rows. When I was in the mountains of Nepal, I observed the farmers growing corn one spindly stalk spaced 1 meter (approximately 3 feet) apart from the next spindly stalk, with the next row 1 meter away. Through the interpreter I asked why they space and plant their crops this way. The answer, as you can probably guess, was "That's the way we've always done it. My father taught me, and that's the way his father taught him."

Just think of all the good that will be accomplished when Square Foot/Meter Gardening is adopted all over the world. It will allow families to grow five times as much for their own use, thereby improving their health through better nutrition; family life will improve with the new abundance. It will draw families closer together as they become involved in a viable and productive project, and they can sell the excess at market. The woman of the family is our primary target for this project, as she is most concerned with the children's nutrition.

"Your method has given me the confidence to try veggies again after a few feeble attempts."

—*Anne from Florida*

Certified SFG Teachers

We hold workshops to train teachers and people who want to help others learn this simple, easy, inexpensive method that anyone, anywhere in the world can do. Just think—what if every woman in the world started just one Square Foot/Meter Garden? Those nine crops could improve the nutrition of her children; many could even expand by planting more gardens for larger harvests and even to grow cash crops. One of our trainees who took our course for certification then went on a mission to teach schoolchildren music at orphanages in an African country. At the same time, she started many SFG projects; her stories of success were heartwarming and inspiring.

Garden of Eden

After enjoying three very productive years with our SFG Display Gardens at Thanksgiving Point, Utah, we had to make a decision because developers were going to build a new building where our gardens were located. Rather than move the gardens to another location, I decided it was time to get away for a sabbatical to do some planning and writing and discovered the beautiful, small mountain community of Eden, Utah. I intended to only stay and write for a few months.

Knowing I would need some clerical help, I placed an ad in the local newspaper and received an overwhelming response from people wanting to help with SFG. Those initial few months stretched into years, and Eden became an appropriately named home base for spreading SFG throughout the world. Through the development of the Square Foot Gardening website and e-mail contacts, the world has literally become my next-door neighbor.

The Story Goes On And On

Recently, a representative from Guadalajara, Mexico, e-mailed asking for one of our representatives to visit and advise him in the development of a large urban SFG project that would teach and enable women to help their families. A really big and impressive project has been started in Sri Lanka. Others have recently written from Ukraine, Mongolia, Egypt, Iraq, Jordan, and Africa requesting training in the SFG method because they see and know what a great difference it can make in their respective countries.

I receive reports from successful SFG projects throughout the world. Such a report came from one of our certified teachers, a professor from Tennessee, along with photos of her international project in Ecuador. Letters come from people in Switzerland, France, Germany, Spain, Argentina, and China volunteering to help translate our website and book into different languages.

The viewer comments sent to our website at **www.squarefoot gardening.com** are phenomenal and the stories are not only heart-warming, but some are very funny. One lady said the only good thing she got in her divorce was my SFG book! Another told of the family bond that was forged as he sat with his father (now deceased) watching my PBS TV show in the early '80s. He still has his father's original book. An entire SFG generation has passed by since I started. Boy, am I getting that old? And now in the electronic age, we have the website and e-mail to replace the TV show and snail mail. Back then, we offered a free garden tips flyer and a packet of seeds (my favorite, marigolds) if viewers sent in a SASE. Do you younger gardeners know what that stands for? Ask your parents. We received ten thousand letters and sold one thousand books every week. What a hectic, exciting experience! But now that's all history, and it's time for an **all new SFG book** for a new generation of gardeners.

Why an All New Square Foot Gardening Book Now?

The answer is simple—I have made so many new improvements to the original basic SFG method. Most of these improvements are so major they make the first SFG book obsolete. Just look at the next page and see why All New Square Foot Gardening can help you with your garden!

SFG, New and Improved

Ten Major New Improvements to the
Original Square Foot Garden Method

1. *New Location*—Close to the House
2. *New Direction*—Up, Not Down
3. *New Soil*—Mel's Mix
4. *New Depth*—Only 6 Inches Deep
5. *No Fertilizer*—You Don't Need It
6. *New Boxes*—Above the Ground
7. *New Aisles*—Comfortable Width
8. *New Grids*—Prominent and Permanent
9. *New Idea*—Don't Waste Seeds
10. *New Opportunities*—Tabletop Gardens

All New Square Foot Gardening offers ten new major improvements to the original SFG method. Now, with these improvements, **anyone** can be a successful gardener. Yes, it's true; this improved gardening method makes gardening even easier than before. You're going to love every one of these improvements.

You will now be able to reduce the size of your SFG so much that you can locate it close to your house for better care and more enjoyment. You'll never have to dig up your existing soil anymore as you now build your new garden on top of it. No more hard work or heavy-duty tools needed. All you'll need is 6 inches of a perfect soil mix from three common ingredients available everywhere. This mix never needs changing and no fertilizer is ever needed using this natural, organic method.

You'll use bottomless boxes made from common lumber, have aisles that are wide enough to comfortably move about in, and each box will have a permanent grid for that unique SFG look and use. You'll use a minimum of seeds, so you won't have to buy new packets every year. Best of all, some of your boxes can have bottoms so you can move them or place them at tabletop or railing heights for easier care and unique locations.

New Location—Close to the House

Single-Row Gardens Are Too Big

One of the biggest problems of single-row and bed gardens is their size. They're big! They take up so much room that they are usually located way out back. That usually meant it was out of sight, resulting in out of mind. It became less and less tended as the year went on. But, guess what still grew? **Weeds!** And these pesky plants can quickly inundate and choke out your crops. Without your attention they'll take over the garden.

No More

All that has been changed for the better. SFG takes only 20 percent of the space of a single-row garden. That means it can be located much closer to the house where it will get more attention and care, resulting in a better-looking garden and a more usable harvest.

Split It Up for Best Location

In addition, your garden doesn't have to be all in one place. You no longer have to rototill or water one big garden area all at once. You can split up your SFG so that a box or two are located next to the kitchen door, while more boxes can be located elsewhere in the yard. Small, individual garden boxes allow you much more flexibility in determining location. Now your garden can be located near where you walk and sit, or where you can view it from the house. It can even be located in a patio or pool setting, where you relax. Your SFG becomes a companion rather than a burden.

The key to success of the All New Square Foot Gardening method is to avoid the poor qualities of local soil by building up rather than digging down.

New Direction—Up, Not Down!

Build Up, Don't Dig Down

The second improvement involves locating your garden **on top** of your existing soil rather than digging **down**. Most of our readers complain about the terrible soil in their areas. In fact, as I lecture around the country and the world, the question I hear most is, "What can we do about our local soil? It is so hard to work and garden in." The original Square Foot Gardening book explained how to dig down 6 inches and improve your existing soil by adding equal amounts of really good ingredients. Even though you had to do that only the first year and it produced a fairly good soil, people complained that it was still a lot of work involving heavy tools and a great deal of effort. Everyone wants a simple, easy way to garden. So, back to the drawing board.

This got me to thinking. Could I find a better way? So, I asked myself, why do we really need to improve our existing soil if it's so bad? Couldn't we just start with a perfect soil mix aboveground and eliminate the need to ever dig up or improve our existing backyard soil? You probably could if your garden wasn't so big . . . but hey, SFG isn't big. In fact, it's one-fifth the size of conventional gardens. So, if we could find a perfect soil mix, there would be no more digging and no more tilling. Doesn't that make a lot of sense? It became possible with All New Square Foot Gardening to have a very condensed no-work gardening method and never have to be concerned again about what kind of soil you have in your yard. Wow!

No Sweat

Just think of the implications if you forget about trying to improve your existing soil. It no longer matters what kind of soil you have! Use the time you save to start a compost pile instead. If you start with a perfect soil mix, it will save a lot of time and money. You don't have to have your soil analyzed anymore, and you don't have to have a pH test made . . . you don't even have to know what pH is! You don't have to buy any heavy tools or go to the expense of having someone rototill your garden every single year. You don't have to buy special ingredients to loosen your clay soil or solidify your sandy soil. And most importantly, you no longer have to do any hard work. You'll have to find another way to get some exercise—so go mow the lawn. This major advance in home gardening changes all of the rules of gardening and eliminates all of the hard work and undesirable parts of single-row gardens. Hey, gardening can be fun now!

So, if you are not going to use your existing soil but instead use a perfect soil mix, what is it and how and where do you get it?

New Soil—Mel's Mix

What's In It?

There are three characteristics of a perfect growing mix. First of all, it's lightweight, so it is easy to work with and easy for plants to grow in. Next, it is nutrient-rich and has all the minerals and trace elements that plants need without adding fertilizers. Finally, it holds moisture, yet drains well.

After many experiments, I found that three of my favorite ingredients made the perfect mix when combined in equal portions:

- $^1/_3$ **Peat Moss**—Available at any garden center or supermarket.

- $^1/_3$ **Vermiculite**—Buy the coarse grade in large 4-cubic-foot bags at any garden center or home improvement store. Phone ahead to be sure it's available in that size.

- $^1/_3$ **Blended Compost**—If you don't have your own compost operation, then buy bags of compost at the garden center to get started. Then, start your own compost pile as soon as possible. I'll explain some simple steps for foolproof composting later in the book. However, one word of caution here: You **must** have a blended compost, so don't buy all the same kind. Pick out one bag of this and one bag of that. But, more about that in Chapter 5.

What Do These Ingredients Do?

All three of these ingredients are natural—not manufactured. They all drain well, so there are no puddles to waterlog the plant roots; but they also hold large amounts of moisture so the plants will grow well. This mix is a pleasure to work with, has a light fluffy texture, and smells good.

The first two ingredients have no nutrients, but the last—compost—is loaded with all the nutrients and minerals that you could imagine. Compost is the most important ingredient of the three, and making your own is good for both the environment and the garden. This is about as organic as you can get.

If you don't think this perfect soil mix will work in the garden, ask yourself, "What do professional greenhouse growers use for growing crops on their benches? Do they go out and dig up the fields for soil?" Of course not. Professional growers mix up a perfect potting soil from several other ingredients and never use local outside soil.

When you buy a windowbox at the store, what do you fill it with—your yard soil? Of course not. You buy a bag of perfect potting soil. So why can't we do the same for our vegetable garden? Well, there are two reasons:

One, no one ever thought of it—and **two,** it would be prohibitively expensive for the typical single-row garden that everyone has been using all of these years.

So, how can we do it now? Because SFG reduces the garden size down to only 20 percent (that's one-fifth as large), so it is now possible to consider using a perfect soil from the very start. An additional reason is found in the next major improvement to Square Foot Gardening.

 ## New Depth—Only 6 Inches Deep

"Go deep," they said. "Don't bother," I said.

For years, experts said your garden soil had to be improved at least 12 inches deep; some even said 18 inches. But my experiments were proving otherwise, especially when I used good homemade compost as one-third of the mix. I asked myself, "If six inches of perfect soil is good enough for windowboxes and commercial greenhouse benches, why not in backyard gardens?" And why dilute it by adding the mix to poor existing soil? Why not use this perfect soil mix in your garden and forget all about the soil underneath? Well, the experts still pooh-poohed the idea. But guess what? **It works!** Of course, everyone realizes that you couldn't do that in a huge, old-fashioned, single-row garden or even in raised bed gardening, but it can easily be done in a small-space Square Foot Garden!

Can you really grow vegetables and flowers in only 6 inches of soil regardless of how good it is? I've been doing it for the last ten years in my display and home garden, and it really works. Of course in my lectures when I mention the 6 inches, I can see the audience squirming in their seats, heads shaking and hands rising with the usual question, "How can you grow long carrots or potatoes in just 6 inches of soil?" It's a good question, so we developed a special feature of SFG where you build a 1-foot × 1-foot box one foot tall for long root crops.

Why only 6 inches deep? Why not be safer and go 12 inches deep? The main reason is there is no need to do so. In addition, it is much cheaper, easier, and less work. Just think—it is one-half of the cost and one-half of the work, so why double the depth? But if you're still skeptical go ahead and use your time and money to go 12 inches deep, but it's really not necessary.

> "We owe much of our love of gardening to the simplicity of SFG."
>
> —*Manja from Oregon*

The next question is, "How come all of the experts have been so wrong for so long?" It is not that they were wrong, it is just everyone in the garden industry had trouble thinking outside the box or even questioning all the traditional methods. Stuck in a rut they were and in a single-row rut at that!

Here's another startling revelation I am going to make. It is going to shock and dismay the gardening world, but you are going to love it.

No Fertilizer—You Don't Need It

Square Foot Gardening needs no fertilizer **ever!** How can that be? After all, the gardening industry is built on using fertilizer. The original SFG book explained all about fertilizer—organic and chemical types—how to measure and rate it; all about NPK and what that means; and the list goes on and on. That was necessary because at that time we were just improving our existing soils, and they still needed fertilizer. All the experts agreed. But my own experiments and thoughts about an **all new out-of-the-box** idea of not improving your existing soil but rather of starting with a perfect soil mix was working so well that I began to consider another new idea—that you don't need to add fertilizer. The compost was providing all of the nutrients and trace elements the plants needed. Besides, compost was all-natural and couldn't burn or harm the plants. The proof of the pudding was to just look at my garden. It was one of the best gardens I have ever had and has remained so ever since.

This was when I was able to simplify my original book's formula for the perfect soil mix to only three ingredients: $1/3$ each of peat moss, vermiculite, and blended compost, and completely eliminate the use and expense of fertilizer. So much simpler than the original one-page formula and what a savings!

Well, again, all the experts pooh-poohed the idea and still do, but guess what? **It works!** I haven't used any kind of fertilizer in my home, display, or demonstration gardens for more than ten years. If you go to our website at **www.squarefootgardening.com,** you'll see how bountiful and beautiful the gardens look. And this is not just gardening the first year but year after year after year.

Just think—**no more tilling, no more digging, and no more fertilizer!** The only thing we ever add to our soil is a little more compost. Is this great or what?

Now all we need is some way to hold or contain our aboveground 6 inches of perfect soil mix. So, how about a box?

New Boxes—Above the Ground

I think having your garden contained in a box adds uniformity and structure, not only to your garden but to your life. Once limits are placed on almost anything, you will find it much easier to take care of and therefore you will be more comfortable with it and enjoy it more.

The basic 4×4-foot bottomless boxes are easy to build out of common lumber, bricks, blocks, or even stone. These small boxes, filled with the perfect soil mix, will grow five times as much as the same space in a single-row garden. So, you don't need many of the boxes. There are no weeds to hoe. No existing soil to till. Why, once your boxes are built and your perfect soil is added, there is virtually no work at all.

If you place the box on top of the existing ground, you eliminate all of the usual gardening concerns and work of improving your existing soil. It also eliminates the great deal of gardening knowledge that you would need if you were going to be concerned with using your existing soil. You'll see as we go along that there are so many advantages of not using your existing soil. You'll wonder why no one ever thought of it before. The 4×4-foot boxes have been chosen because it's a size you can walk around and easily reach into to tend your plants; this eliminates the need for stepping on the growing to dig or loosen it.

Once you build the basic 4×4 SFG box with rotated corners, add six inches of Mel's Mix, and add the square foot grid. Now, you're ready to plant.

See how everything in SFG is interrelated and works so well together?

For bigger gardens, you can always put some of the boxes end to end to create a 4×8-foot or a 4×12-foot garden box that you will still be able to walk around, yet reach in. If your box is located next to a wall, fence, or building, keep the boxes only two feet wide so you can reach all the way to the back. They can be any length. Boxes can be made from any type of wood. The best is **free** wood that is found at a construction site. Just ask the foreman of the project if you can have the scrap 2×6-inch boards. If you are going to buy your lumber, boxes can be made from pine or fir for the least cost, or cedar or redwood for longer lasting use. If you decide to treat or paint the wood, be careful not to paint inside the boxes where the Mel's Mix comes into contact with the wood; you don't want anything harmful to leach into the soil. I do not recommend using pretreated wood for the same reason.

New Aisles—Comfortable Width

The width of your aisles is another improvement I have made for the All New Square Foot Gardening method. This is more important for comfort, safety, and looks, than for efficiency. If you notice the garden on the cover of the original Square Foot Gardening book, there were no boxes and the aisles were 1×12-inch boards separating the 4×4-foot areas. I designed it that way to be the most space-efficient but, as someone once said, "This is one time when Mel was too efficient!" But the wood was free, so hey, can you blame me?

Straight and Narrow

The 12-inch wide board was difficult to maneuver on, and you had to keep a pretty good balance to stay upright. I found that the average gardener needs to have more room to move about on than those 12 inches. In addition, you couldn't get close to each 4×4-foot planting area if you wanted to use a wheelbarrow, garden cart, or harvest basket. Can you just picture two people working in that garden with 12-inch wide paths, and one says to the other, "Excuse me, I need to get through." Can you imagine the answer to that?

The Ideal Width

So what is the ideal aisle width? Two feet is still a little tight, so I recommend a minimum of three feet between your boxes. It turned out that for accessibility, kneeling, working, and harvesting, the ideal distance was 3 or even 4 feet between boxes. In fact, if your garden has several boxes, you can vary the aisles. Play around with some ideas on paper—then, once your boxes are built (and before you fill them with soil, I should add), you can move them about until you get them just right. Think of it as arranging furniture in your yard.

Dress It Up

The aisle space between your boxes can be left in grass or covered with any type of ground cover. In our TV show, we tried all sorts of things to create some very interesting looking aisles. At other times, we just removed any weeds or grass, then laid down weed cloth and covered it with materials that were comfortable for walking on such as crushed stone, compost, or ground bark.

MEL SAYS...

Forget what the experts have been telling us for years, fill your boxes with just 6 inches of Mel's Mix, add a grid, and start planting! You won't be sorry; in fact, you'll be amazed at the results.

8 New Grids—Prominent and Permanent

When I wrote the first book on Square Foot Gardening more than twenty-five years ago, I advocated laying out a 12×12-inch grid for the garden. Then, in my travels around the country, I heard a lot of people say, "Oh, I do Square Foot Gardening," or "I have a Square Foot Garden." But when I went to see them, the size was right but they had no grid!

In our introductory film, we show the people in our class how a 4×4-foot garden looks without a grid and ask them, "How many plants could you plant there? How many different crops?" They draw a blank because it looks like a small area that isn't going to contain very much. As soon as we lay down the grid, they suddenly light up and say, "Aha! I see! Sixteen spaces, so it'll take sixteen different crops! Later, as soon as one square is harvested, I can add a trowel full of compost and replant that square foot with a different crop without disturbing anything else around it." Bingo! They see the light.

See how the grid defines a Square Foot Garden? Without a grid, it's hard to visualize the harvest.

There are many, many interrelated reasons for the "different crop in every Square Foot" rule, and you will see and understand these as we go along. They deal with nutrients used, limiting over-ambitious planting, staggered harvests, weed and pest control, beauty of the garden, companion planting, simplification of crop rotation, cutting planting time in half, and many more factors that result in a very unusual and innovative gardening system. When you have no grid, your garden has no character. If you're having visitors over, they may not even notice your garden if it's laid out in plain beds. But if it's a Square Foot Garden with very prominent and visible grids, they will say, "Hey, what's that in your yard? It looks great!"

Grid Materials

In the past, whenever I used string or twine as a grid, it eventually got dirty, rotted, and finally broke. In addition, you had to drive in nails to tie the string to, and it just never looked good. I talked with many others who had the same bad experience so I experimented with all kinds of different materials for making grids. If I could condense thirty years of experience into my current advice, it would be—don't use string or any other floppy material. A firm, rigid, prominent, and visual grid permanently laid on every one of your boxes will make all the difference in the world as others see it but mostly in how you use and enjoy your garden.

With a very visible grid, your garden takes on a unique character. It will not only look spectacular, but you'll be able to immediately visualize your planting squares. **Without a grid, your garden is not a Square Foot Garden.**

New Idea—Don't Waste Seeds

New Seed Planting Idea

When I first started gardening, I found the traditional method of pouring out an entire packet of seeds along a single row was so wasteful that I couldn't believe that's the way we've always done it. Didn't the pioneers have to carry their own seeds all the way across the country? They couldn't order a new batch over the Internet from a seed company every year, could they? Didn't they teach everyone to be frugal and not wasteful? Why would anyone tell us to waste a whole packet of seeds along a long, lonely, single row, especially knowing that we would have to go back and thin out 95 percent of the sprouted plants in order to leave only one plant every few inches. Did no one ever think, "Let's just plant a few seeds every 3, 4, or 6 inches?" I guess it took someone outside of the garden industry to think of it.

When your seeds sprout from the pinch of seeds you planted in your squares, snip out all but one of them.

In the first SFG book, I advocated single seed planting at the proper spacing for that particular plant, but many people found it tedious and even difficult, especially with small, unusually shaped seeds. Besides, as someone once teased me and said, "If a packet of leaf lettuce contains one thousand seeds and I only plant four in each square foot, how old will I be before it is time to buy another packet?" She'll have to leave her seeds in her will!

So back to the drawing board I went. How about just a few seeds in each hole—just a pinch of seeds? After testing this idea with many people and checking their dexterity and ability to pick up just a pinch (two or three seeds), this seemed to be the answer.

A Snip, Not a Tug

But I was against thinning—that's when you pull out all the seedlings except the one plant you want to grow to maturity. Thinning is a lot

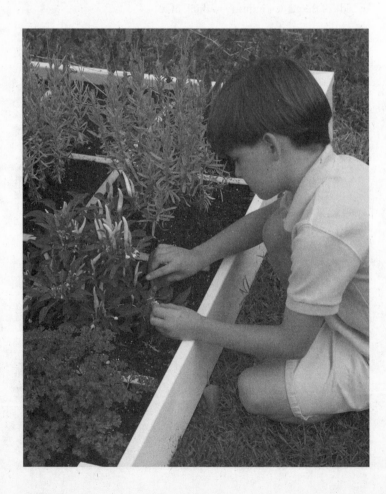

of work and also seems to disturb the roots of the remaining plant, and that's not good. But then I thought of an absolutely perfect solution. If you plant just a few seeds—a pinch—in each hole and two or three seedlings come up, you just take a pair of scissors and snip off all but the strongest one. That eliminates any disturbance of the plant you want to keep, and you're not tempted to replant the others. The only thing you need to do is just muster the courage to make that initial snip and it's all over.

So now we've been able to improve the single-seed planting and, at the same time, end up with one strong plant in each location, which is just what we wanted. At the same time we're not wasting a lot of seeds. After planting that square foot, put the packet in safe storage, and if stored properly that packet will be good next year, and the year after, and the year after. Many seeds last up to five years if stored properly. (So, how come no one ever told us that before?)

New Opportunities—Tabletop Gardens

Make Them Portable

Now that we no longer need to improve our existing soil—and SFG takes up only 20 percent of the space for 100 percent of the harvest—and we need only 6 inches of lightweight soil mix, we can build a 4×4-foot box, and add a plywood bottom drilled with drainage holes. This means you can carry it to any location you want, even moving it to suit weather, climate, an event, a situation, or even a person's needs, abilities, or disabilities. If the size or weight seems too much for you to handle, think about using a 3×3-foot, a 2×2-foot, or even a 2×4-foot box for ease in moving.

James, Bring Out the Good Boxes

Smaller sized SFG boxes can become wonderful patio boxes, and it's even possible to plant several so there is always one or two with flowers in full bloom or salad crops ready for harvest. The rest can be kept somewhere less visible. With a system of rotation, there will always be a few garden boxes ready to bring out to show off. There's nothing like the visual impact of a beautifully planted box filled with vegetables, flowers, and/or herbs. If you're giving a talk or doing a presentation on gardening, the "seeing is believing" technique will cinch your talk. And just think, you won't have to answer the usual question about SFG, like "How on earth can you grow a garden in only 6 inches of soil?" Or, "How can you grow without fertilizer?" Now, you just point and smile!

REASONS TO MOVE YOUR PORTABLE SFG BOX

WEATHER—To protect it from:
- Frost
- Thundershowers
- Hurricanes
- Hail
- Snow
- Wind
- Heavy rain
- Intense sun

CLIMATE—Move your SFG box for:
- More shade for a spring crop as the weather gets hotter
- More sun in early spring
- More shade in summertime in desert areas

EVENTS—Move it to:
- Enhance or decorate for a poolside party or barbeque
- Behind the garage for a start-up nursery

SITUATIONS—Place the box:
- On a tabletop for a sit-down gardener
- In the garage if you're expecting extreme weather
- On the deck to clear the yard for a football game

PERSONS—You can:
- Take it to Grandma's for a birthday gift
- Take it to school for show-and-tell
- Take it to class for teaching SFG
- Take it to school for the science fair

Best of All

So there you have it—the ten new major improvements to the Square Foot Gardening method. Each one makes the entire system more productive, the work much easier, and the cost of gardening lower. At the same time, the beginner finds gardening much easier to understand.

I think Square Foot Gardening's best feature is that it now makes gardening available to just about anyone you can think of, regardless of their age, circumstance, location, ability, or disability—**anyone, anywhere, can now garden** using the All New Square Foot Gardening method.

Plan Your Garden

This chapter is going to talk about three basic components of Square Foot Gardening.

- Size ▪ Location ▪ Design

Size

Your garden will be laid out in square or rectangular boxes separated by walking aisles. Build your boxes from materials like wood, bricks, or blocks. If you don't like the idea of common wood, which will eventually rot or be eaten by termites, use a more expensive wood like cedar or redwood. You can even use some of the manmade composite "wood" or recycled plastic or vinyl. The wood I like best is **free** wood. You can usually get it from any construction site, but always ask the foreman first.

THE BIG DILEMMA

Should you first design the layout for your garden, then try to find a spot where it will fit?

OR

First find the best spot for a garden, then design a layout that will fit into that spot?

If you decide to use lumber, you'll be happy to know the advantage of 4×4 gardens is that all lumber comes in 8-foot lengths. Most home improvement centers will cut it in half for you at little or no cost. Your boxes can be made from just about any material except treated wood because the chemicals used to treat the wood are not something you want leaching into your garden.

How Much Is Enough?

If you're figuring a SFG for an adult, remember that:

1. One 4×4 Square Foot Garden box (equal to 16 square feet) will supply enough produce to make a salad for one person every day of the growing season.

2. One more 4×4 box will supply the daily supper vegetables for that person.

3. Just one more 4×4 box will supply that person with extra of everything for preserving, special crops, showing off, or giving away.

So, each adult needs one, two, or three large boxes of 4×4, depending on how much they want. In square feet, that is 16, 32, or 48 square feet.

Salad   *Daily Vegetables*   *Preserving*

If you're figuring a SFG for a child, remember that:

1. One 3×3 Square Foot Garden box (equal to 9 square feet) will supply enough produce to make a salad for one child every day of the growing season.

2. One more 3×3 box will supply supper vegetables for that child every day.

3. Just one more 3×3 box will supply the child with extra of everything for show-and-tell or science projects at school, special crops, showing off, or giving away. So, each child needs one, two, or three small boxes of 3×3, depending on how much they will eat. In square feet, that's 9, 18, or 27 square feet.

Suggestion: Since the kids will grow into teenagers, you may just want to make everyone's box a 4×4. On the other hand, different sizes make the garden look interesting and more personable. The 3×3 can later on be stacked on top of a 4×4 to start a pyramid garden—but more about designing your garden later.

Your Family—Your Garden

According to surveys of homeowners, the average conventional single-row garden measures 20 feet wide by 35 feet long, which equals 700 square feet. To grow the same amount, a Square Foot Garden will need only 20 percent or one-fifth of that growing space to equal 140 square feet. That's quite a difference isn't it?

YOUR FAMILY—YOUR GARDEN

Number of Boxes or Square Feet	Salad	Supper	Extra	Total
Mom				
Dad				
Grandpa or Grandma				
Brother				
Sister				
Pets*				
Other				

*Well, some dogs eat veggies and cats love catnip.
**You can enter the number of boxes—big for adults, small for kids—
or square feet.**

Down to Size

Whenever I'm giving a lecture I like to illustrate the difference between a conventional garden and a Square Foot Garden. I'll walk down the middle of whatever room we're in and, standing in the center, stretch out my arms sideways, as I say, "If this whole room were our garden, when you switch to Square Foot Gardening, you'll no longer need everything on this side." That cuts the room in half. Then I turn to the side that remains, cut it in half with my arms again, and say, "Everything on that side we don't need." That cuts that half in half again. And then I add, "That's still too much room. We can still cut down this remaining corner even more so we end up with only 20 percent of the total room. We can grow as much in this size of a Square Foot Garden as we previously could in this entire room."

 A TYPICAL FAMILY WOULD NEED

For easy multiplying, round off the adults' measurements of 16, 32, and 48 to 15, 30, and 50 square feet per person. For children, you can round off the 9, 18, and 27 to 10, 20, and 30 square feet. To figure the area in square feet compared to boxes, try this. A family of two adults plus one teenager plus one child needs:

(2 + 1) × 50 = 150 square feet
+ 1 × 20 = 20 square feet
Total: 170 square feet

Try it in the room you're in right now and see if you aren't impressed. You suddenly begin to think of the reduced amount of work, equipment, supplies, and fencing. Then you begin to see many of the advantages of being able to locate the garden where you wish and all the possibilities in your yard. Visualizing the great difference of space needed for a Square Foot Garden is really the first step in learning and appreciating the entire system. Then you can begin to take advantage of all the other attributes you will discover with SFG.

All That in One Box

How much salad could you pick every day from this little garden? More than you can imagine. So as an illustration, I've listed below examples of what you can harvest from just one 4×4 box in one spring season:

 ■ one head of cabbage

 ■ one head of broccoli

 ■ one head of cauliflower

 ■ four heads of romaine lettuce

 ■ four heads of red lettuce

 ■ four heads leaf lettuce, then sixteen scallions

 ■ four heads of salad lettuce

 ■ five pounds sugar peas

 ■ eight bunches of Swiss chard

 ■ nine bunches of spinach, then nine turnips

 ■ sixteen small, ball carrots

 ■ sixteen beets, plus four bunches beet greens

 ■ sixteen long carrots

 ■ thirty two radishes

Start Small

Once you decide on the final size and layout of your garden, keep in mind you don't have to build the entire garden right at the start. Try a three-phase plan instead.

If you build and plant just one-third of your ultimate garden boxes and grow for one season—for example, the spring season—you can then see how much you'll harvest and see if you've correctly judged the amount you really need. Then you can go into phase two, or the summer crop, and build more boxes according to your layout or master plan. At the end of the summer crop, move on to phase three, building more boxes if you still need them, to prepare for planting a fall crop.

Yes, it's okay to lay out the whole area and to design it for the ultimate, depending on how big your family is and how much you think you want to harvest. Just don't do everything the first season. I've seen so many people start out too ambitiously, and they become overwhelmed because they underestimate how much they can actually grow in such a small area. Their gardens are actually larger than they need so there is more to take care of—and all while they're learning a new system. Take it easy and start small.

If you have a single-row garden and don't really want to give it up yet, I suggest taking one small corner of your old-fashioned garden and planting it in just one or two 4×4 boxes, mix the correct soil (don't just shovel your existing soil into the boxes no matter how good you think it is), put down the grid, and try planting this way. Next year, I'll bet you'll probably be ready to convert your entire garden into a SFG.

Overall Size of the Boxes

Once you decide on the overall size and number of boxes, the next step is to determine the dimension of the aisles. We'll cover this in more detail later, but for now you can figure on a 3-foot aisle between all 4-foot boxes. You could also decide now if you want to join several boxes together end to end to create a rectangular box of 4×8, or 4×12. This will save a lot of yard space but you may not like the look or you may find walking around a long box inconvenient. I would never make a box longer than 16 feet or you'll end up trying to cross it in the middle and then—whoops!—there you are, stepping in your garden. I hope no one saw you! If you are going to be putting some boxes against a fence or wall and can't walk all around to reach in, those boxes should be only 2 feet wide. Everyone wants to make them 3 feet wide (I will never know why) but then they always come back and complain it was too wide because they couldn't reach in that far.

Don't Forget the Aisles

The whole idea of Square Foot Gardening is to walk around your garden boxes and reach in to tend your plants. This way, the soil never gets packed down and you eliminate digging it up to loosen it again. In fact, the only tool you really need once you fill your boxes with Mel's Mix is a small hand trowel. (It doesn't have to be the strong, expensive kind from Sweden. The one dollar variety works just fine and can last a lifetime.)

So how wide should your aisles be? It depends a lot on how much room you have and what kind of a look you want for your garden. If you're going to have many boxes—remember, we suggest you begin using only a small number because you can always add more later—

> "Gardening has always seemed too overwhelming. Now with your method, I can't wait to start."
> —*Alejiendra from Venezuela*

MEL SAYS...

THINK TWICE

Your aisles should be 3 feet wide. I would caution against 2-foot wide aisles because once the plants grow, some cascade over the sides or get bushy. Those 2-foot aisles begin to shrink down to maybe just 18 or even 12 inches. At the beginning, when nothing is planted or growing, it's hard to imagine what it will look like in midsummer with everything growing like crazy and taking up a lot more space. Pretty soon you're sorry that you made the aisle so narrow. But by then, it's too late to move the boxes. Since SFG takes up so little room, why crowd all your boxes together? The more spacious your All New Square Foot Garden is, the more time you are likely to spend there enjoying it.

you may want to have, for example, a center aisle that is 4 feet wide so you can easily get in with a garden cart or wheelbarrow, or so several people can walk down the aisle at once. (Hey, how about a garden party or a wedding?)

Draw It Up

Once you get a rough idea of how much space you'll need, make a quick sketch more or less to scale. You don't need graph paper (unless you're a designer or want to use it); just draw the 3-foot aisles slightly smaller than the 4-foot boxes. Now you're ready to tour your property looking for nice open areas near the house. Later in this chapter we'll discuss design in more detail.

Location

There are five major things to look for when touring your property for a SFG location. Use these as a test for the area you're considering for your All New Square Foot Garden. (Remember, convenience is king so make sure you follow Rule 1.)

1. Place it close to the house for convenience.

2. Pick an area that gets six to eight hours of sunshine daily.

3. Stay clear of trees and shrubs where roots and shade may interfere.

4. The area should not puddle after a heavy rain.

5. The existing soil is not really important, since you won't be using it.

1. Close to the House

With the All New Square Foot Gardening Method, you have so many more places to put your garden than ever before.

Keep in mind foot traffic and sites where you will often notice and enjoy your garden. If your SFG is near traffic paths, you'll walk past the garden more often, hence take better care of it (remember— no need to change into gardening clothes, or run and get some tools). This means it will always look nice and the end result will be that you'll enjoy it more as will every other member of the family. (Chapter 10 covers different locations like hillsides or heavily wooded areas.)

I Can See Clearly Now

When you think about observing your garden, consider where you can frequently see it—especially from inside the house. What room are you in the most? Can you see the garden from there? The reason is not only for your pleasure but for protection. If it is close, you will see problems (like deer, wilting plants, a neighbor's dog or cat) when they begin rather than hours later after all the damage is done.

Remember the Square Foot Garden way is to treat your plants just like you treat your children or grandchildren, and you know you would be glancing out the window at them. I believe that every plant out there is constantly seeking your attention by saying, "Look at me, look at my new blossom, look how big I'm getting." Isn't that just like children?

Placement of your Square Foot Garden opens up so many doors to the way you care for, enjoy, appreciate, and harvest it. Plus you'll show it off more often and get the whole family involved. It's even possible to split up your garden and place some of your boxes in different locations for perhaps a different visual effect or a different purpose.

MEL SAYS...

REMEMBER THE OLD NURSERY RHYME?

One for the blackbird.
One for the mouse.
One for the rabbit.
And one for the house.

So they're suggesting you plant four times as much as what you really want or need. Well, that's cute, but what a waste of resources and energy.

2. Sunlight

The next thing to consider in selecting a location is sunlight. Growing plants need sunlight. How much they need depends on the type of plant. In general, large-flowering or fruiting plants need a lot—at least eight hours a day. These types of plants are referred to as a "summer crop" or "warm-weather plants" and include most of the favorite things that people grow, such as tomatoes, peppers, squash, beans, and sunflowers.

In determining the amount of sunlight an area receives, keep in mind that it changes throughout the year with the seasons. In early spring and again in late fall the sun is lower in the sky than in the summertime. And of course, there are not as many hours of light in the day in the spring and fall as there are in the summer.

If You Only Have Shade

If you have shady conditions and no other place to locate your garden, you can still have a thriving garden but you'll have a limited selection of crops to grow. So, obviously, you'd stay away from the tomatoes, peppers, and squash and plant the root and leaf crops like radishes, spinach, and lettuce. Of course, there are many flowers and herbs that love shade, so check with your local nursery if you are in this situation.

Too Much Sun

Sometimes you might have a location that gets full sun all day long, from sunup to sundown. That would actually be too much for some of the cool weather and leafy crops, as well as many flowers. Of course, with a big, huge garden there's not much you can do. But with a Square Foot Garden, it's very easy to provide shade by building a simple support and covering the 4×4 box with some shade cloth. That's all covered in Chapter 4.

"I *want to convert my entire garden to your method.*"
—*Guy from Utah*

3. Avoid Trees and Shrubs

When choosing your SFG location, stay clear of trees and shrubs for two reasons. The first is shade as we just discussed. Second, if they sense a well-watered perfect soil nearby, these roots will come straight as an arrow into your soil. If that's the only location you have, then there is a way to counteract that situation. Put a plywood bottom on your boxes and raise them up off the ground. You can raise them up by just putting a brick under each corner and one in the center. Or you can use a cement block, or even two blocks and build little piers and have it as a garden you sit down beside to harvest. Then, of course, the tree's roots won't even know that the garden is there. This is a nice way to have a shade garden right under a tree along with a bench or a few lawn chairs.

Keep in mind that shrubs are just as bad as trees as far as providing shade and root interference. Most shrubs are more shallow-rooted than trees. Keep in mind, too, that as trees and shrubs grow, their shade will increasingly cover a larger area.

4. No Puddles, Please

Roots will drown in accumulated and stagnant water, so you don't want to locate your SFG in an area that holds water after a rain. The materials in Mel's Mix, though they drain well and hold a lot of moisture, will soak up all the water in a standing puddle and your plant roots will be harmed. Areas that puddle also promise mud in the aisles, which makes gardening less fun.

If you have no other place and can't drain the area, then of course you could fill in the low area with sand to raise your box slightly and/or you could again put a bottom on it and raise it up with stones, bricks, cinder blocks, or something similar.

MEL SAYS...

Once you choose the spot, you'll love Square Foot Gardening for so many reasons. It's simple and easy to understand. It's quick and practical to do. It has every benefit you can think of. It fits anywhere in an existing or planned landscape; anyone can do it regardless of abilities. It costs very little. It requires few tools and equipment. And the best part of all is that you don't have to be an expert gardener!!

5. Existing Soil—Who Cares?

When you're choosing a location, it doesn't really matter about the condition of your existing soil. Many of the other gardening books tell you how to go around the yard and dig test holes and see what kind of soil you have. Sometimes you're even supposed to make a percolation test, in which you have to dig a hole, fill it with water, see how long it takes to drain, blah, blah, blah . . . . Or, how about all the unnecessary advice on how to take a soil test and what the results mean? Forget about all that now. You don't have to know about it because we're not going to use your existing soil. We're going to build bottomless boxes above the ground. You can even put your boxes on the pavement or a patio and it won't make any difference.

The Envelope, Please

The best location is where you can see your garden more often from more directions. Things like sunlight and avoiding trees and shrubs are merely precautions to help make your garden more successful. So walk around your yard and think about the best place to locate and enjoy your garden.

Design

Now that you've determined how many boxes you'll have and strolled around your yard to find the best spot(s), it's time to think about design. You can lay out your boxes so they turn corners, even intersect each other, but keep in mind traffic and walking around. Don't make dead ends or narrow places. Keep 3- or 4-foot aisles, and leave bigger areas for chairs, benches, and entranceways. Here is a fun idea: explain to the entire family the basic size and layout then let each member draw up ideas and plans. Maybe everyone could have an area to design, build, and plant. Wouldn't that be a great family project? Then, take a picture and send it to me so we can share all kinds of designs with others.

Line Them Up

You can probably guess that, being a former army officer, I am going to want all the boxes lined up neatly and precisely, even perhaps having them in a row (oh, what an unfortunate word)—excuse me—in a line. I might want the entire area to be a square or at the very least a rectangle . . but that's just me. How about you—do you want a U-shape or an L-shape? Do whatever appeals to you.

Gardens Aren't Just for Yards Anymore

Here's another idea—no matter the season, you can build a SFG box with a plywood bottom and place it on your patio or picnic tabletop near your back door. You may want to use smaller SFG boxes on the patio or deck such as 2×2 or 2×4.

Be Creative

You don't have to be a landscape architect to measure and draw up what you imagine. The design is just as important as the size. You're going to be spending a lot of your time in your SFG—not working or weeding, but just enjoying and relaxing. Be sure to make room for some chairs, a bench, a water fountain, or a bird bath. One of the advantages of a Square Foot Garden is that you have options in how you put it together so that it's perfect for you.

Seeing a picture is so helpful. If you want to see what others have done in their yard with Square Foot Gardening, go to **www.squarefootgardening.com** and click on "Neighborhood Gardens." Everyone likes to see what others have done, so take the garden tour and see which one you like the best. And then let your imagination help you create the Square Foot Garden that is perfect for you.

Building Boxes and Structures

If you like to build things, you are going to love this chapter. A Square Foot Garden can be a lot like working with Erector® sets, Lincoln Logs®, or Legos®. Since SFG grows so much in so little space and is made with readily available materials, the basic box projects outlined in this chapter won't take all your time, space, or money.

Why Boxes?

Just as a reminder, there are several reasons we build boxes for our Square Foot Gardens.

1. **Looks neat and tidy.**
2. **Organizes and simplifies your gardening chores.**
3. **Holds a special soil mix aboveground.**
4. **It's easy to add protective features.**

If your garden is boxed in, it has already-established limits for you. And if you make sure to add a grid, it establishes not only a pattern but a formula for success.

Boxes also hold your perfect soil mix so that it doesn't spill out or wash away in a heavy rainstorm. When garden beds have no borders between plant-growing soil and walkways, there's a greater chance that someone will step into the growing soil—a big no-no for this SFG method.

Let's start with the basic 4×4 SFG box. Examples of box materials that can be used include:

- Natural wood
- Manmade wood
- Recycled plastic
- Vinyl
- Or any other manmade material available in lumber sizes

Recommended Material Size

- 1×6-inch lumber for the most economical, low traffic garden; or
- 2×6-inch lumber for sturdier boxes or heavy traffic garden areas.

> "**S**FG is more than a hobby, it's a movement."
> —Ross from South Carolina

QUICK START GUIDE

MATERIALS

Make sure you've got all you need: four 4-foot 2 × 6-inch boards, 6 four-foot wood lath boards, weed cloth, Mel's Mix, wood screws, a power drill, and your seeds.

PREPARATION

Stack your four boards and pre-drill 3 holes in one end of each board.

ASSEMBLY

Screw 3 large, coarse-thread deck screws through the pre-drilled holes, attaching the boards end-to-end, until you have a complete frame.

Once assembled, move the box to your chosen location, remove grass or weeds, and cover that spot with weed cloth.

COMPLETION

Fill the box with Mel's Mix until it covers the bottom and then water. (Do this three times until your box is full.) Then, add your wood lath grid and plant!

Stack your lumber like steps. Once you drill the top piece, slide the board back to expose the next one.

All types of lumber come in 8-foot lengths and multiples of 2 feet thereafter. Since most SFGs will be 4×4 feet, ask the lumber company to cut your 8-foot-long wood in half when you buy it. They usually do this for free. Then it's easier to take home, quicker to assemble, and eliminates any need for sawing. All types of wood can be used: pine, fir, cedar, or even redwood (which is more expensive but longer-lasting), but don't use treated lumber.

Rotate Corners

When constructing your SFG box, cut all four pieces of your wood sides to the same length, and then rotate the corners to ensure you end up with a square box. If you want a different look than the rotated corners, measure the thickness of the lumber and subtract that from two of the sides and add it to the other two sides so you still end up with a square box. It is not critical that your garden box be exactly 48 inches either inside or outside, but it should be square so each square foot planting area is the same size.

Attach your box with coarse-thread deck screws that are twice as long as the thickness of the lumber. Use three screws per corner. Pre-drill your holes in the first piece of the two pieces you're connecting; the threads will embed themselves into the second.

PENNY PINCHER

My idea of the best kind of wood is free wood. Go to any construction site, tell the foreman you are building a Square Foot Garden, and ask if they have any scrap lumber. Chances are they will be throwing out just what you need. They may even cut it for you if you ask nicely. Then your box is free.

This is an example of corner construction; the side of one board is attached to the end of another, with three deck screws.

Construction Details

Work on a hard surface—like a driveway, pavement, or sidewalk—and keep your frame flat so it won't end up crooked or twisted. When your frame is all screwed together, carry it to the garden area, lay it down, and see how it looks. If you want to preserve the wood, you could use linseed oil. It's also possible to paint or stain the bottom, outside, and top. Leave the inside unpainted so there's no possible contamination to the growing mix.

MEL SAYS...

If you're starting with used lumber and it already has paint on it, you must make sure that it's not old paint, especially if it's peeling or crumbling; some older paints contain lead, which is toxic. You don't want that in your garden. I also don't recommend using pretreated timbers or lumber because it also can leach chemicals.

For proper drainage, drill holes in the plywood bottom of your tabletop garden—one per square foot and one extra in each corner.

Other Box Materials

SFG boxes can also be constructed with brick, cement blocks, prefabricated stone, or large rocks. Stone for your SFG box can be manmade preformed sizes or natural slate, round, riverbed, or any other type of decorative stone that is easy to place and forms an interesting border.

Plywood Bottom

If you decide to create a bottom for your SFG, use plywood sheeting and drill $1/4$-inch drainage holes, one per square foot plus an extra hole in each corner. You attach this bottom by putting it on top of the assembled box sides, screwing it down, then flipping it over so the box sides are sitting on top of the plywood bottom.

Plywood thickness depends on the size of the box. A 2×2 or 2×3 box—anything spanning less than 3 feet—needs ½-inch plywood. Your 4×4-foot boxes need 5/8- or even ¾-inch plywood bottoms. Use the ¾-inch plywood if you are going to move it often. If the box is going to rest on sawhorses or cement blocks and span a large, unsupported distance, it requires thicker plywood. I use regular plywood although some like to spend extra for the longer lasting, but much more expensive, marine or waterproof plywood.

Special Structures

For out-of-season gardening, you can create spring, summer, fall, and/or winter boxes. These are just 4×4 foot standard garden boxes or smaller 2×4 size that can be modified for special uses; we'll explain that in Chapter 9. Depending on the time of year, boxes can be equipped with double decks, extensions, covers, or special modifications to allow a longer growing season. Usually these modifications are weather-related items like covers to shade tender seedlings in the summer or a frost protector either in spring or fall. You will determine the best modifications, depending on your particular weather and environmental conditions.

Railing Boxes

If you have flat railings, it is very easy to set a box right on top of it. For stability, it should be bolted to the wood railing. If you can't bolt your boxes down and you're higher than the first floor, I would place the boxes on the floor. Consider the strength and size of your railing and the surrounding environment, and make sure your railing boxes aren't too big.

You can build a Square Foot Garden box that bolts to your deck railing.

Railing boxes make a very decorative and excellent garden, particularly if you add trailing types of plants that add some color and character. There are various holders sold at home improvement stores that snap onto your railings to accommodate standard-sized boxes. Hang the box over the outside edge, and it won't take up any of your valuable deck space, and, should it drip when you're watering, the water will bypass the deck below. However, if your box is on the inside of the railing, it would be much safer.

Pyramid Boxes

Be creative and make your SFG uniquely yours. Why not get fancy and stack one on top of another to create pyramids? Why would you do that? Because they're spectacular, and they will be the highlight and focal point of your entire garden. Construction is very simple with just a few braces for stability.

Step Up, Young Lady

The next fancy garden layout would be to make a standard 4-foot wide by any length box but every 2 or 4 feet step up by one level. There are many arrangements you could design, and they would be limited only by your imagination. Build them the same way as the corner pyramid with an inside brace for every 4-foot section.

One-foot-square boxes are the perfect size for the steps leading to your front door.

Make Boxes Extra Deep

Making boxes that are extra deep mean they are extra dramatic. I know I've told you that 6 inches of Mel's Mix is enough for all plants, but your garden becomes more dramatic when the container is extra tall. If you decide to build your box taller, just use 8-, 10-, or 12-inch lumber instead of the normal 6 inches. The only drawback is cost. But no matter—you're after a dramatic, spectacular look now. Since the plants don't need more than 6 inches of Mel's Mix, don't spend your money on filling the entire depth with Mel's Mix. Use sand (cheap and available at any home improvement center) on the bottom layer. "I'll just use my existing yard soil," someone says "and save even more money." **Don't!** Most soils don't drain well and have **weed** seeds. Remember weeds? We don't have them anymore in SFG, so if you're going to multiple layers for your garden boxes, fill any space below 6 inches with just ordinary sand.

A Special Box for Carrots, Leeks, and Potatoes

There is one last item that you might want to construct—your high-rise boxes for carrots, leeks, and potatoes. These root crops need deep soil so instead of digging down as in most gardening methods, we take the easy way and build up. Build a 1 × 1-foot box either 6, 9, or 12 inches tall out of plywood or any thin type of lumber. See Chapter 6 for details on planting and growing.

Grids and Materials

Grids are a must. Every box should have its own permanent and prominent grid. I'm so adamant about having a grid on every box I tell people that if your SFG doesn't have a grid, it is not a Square Foot Garden. But with a grid, it's an attractive, unusual, and unique garden. It tells the story of SFG in one glance. In addition it has many unseen benefits, so stick with me on this one and build a grid for all of your boxes.

Blinds

The first Penny Pincher tip is slat-type or Venetian blinds. They come in many widths and lengths, and if you visit a local thrift shop you can usually find a used set at a great price. Find one that's at least 4 feet wide. Cut off the strings and lay out the strips. Trim the ends with a pair of scissors so they fit your box, drill holes at the half and quarter points, and attach them

PENNY PINCHER

INEXPENSIVE GRIDS

I used to search home improvement centers for wood or plastic molding, or strips of any type of material that was straight. But they were expensive. Then I found two materials that are just perfect and cheap.

together with some sort of screw, nail, or snap-fastener. The one problem I've found with blinds is their weight. When you first start your garden in the spring, it's usually windy. Sometimes the blinds blow around a little just because the garden is empty and they have no protection from the wind. One solution is to attach them to the soil with a long galvanized nail at every 12-inch intersection. This helps hold them down so they don't blow away.

Wood Lath

The second inexpensive material is wood lath, which is sold in home improvement centers. Believe it or not, they already come 4 feet long with square ends. Sometimes they're a little crooked, filled with knots, or break easily, so sort through them. But they're very, very inexpensive—less than a quarter each. Once you lay them out and drill holes at the 12-inch intersections, they're very easy to connect together with a nut and bolt or some other type of

Drill a hole through both pieces of wood at each grid intersection.

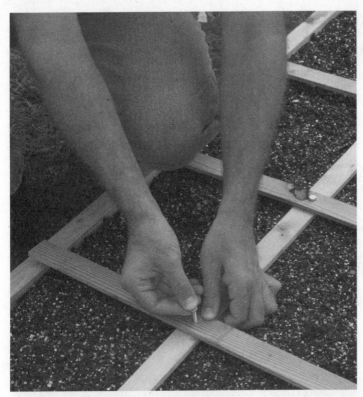

Next, insert some kind of hardware to loosely hold
the grid together.

Drill a hole through the end of the center grids and add 4 deck screws.

Once the grid is attached, your square foot garden is ready for planting.

fastener. Because the wood lath is rigid, it can span from one side of the box to the other side in case your Mel's Mix is not level with the top of the box. Otherwise, it can just lie on top of the soil. If your grid spans across the box sides, keep the grid from moving about by drilling a hole in the ends of the two center slats and screwing them to your wooden box. Some people like to take the wood lath grid up for

MEL SAYS...

Grids need to remain in place during the entire growing season. Remember you're harvesting and replanting each square foot throughout the season. Besides that, you want to make sure everyone notices you have an authentic SFG.

the winter so it doesn't get wet and rot as easily. Unscrew the four screws, fold the grid, and hang it on the garage wall. Put the screws in a plastic bag and hang it up with the grid to keep the screws safe and dry over the winter.

Fun Ideas

You may be able to find other scrap wood strips around. Carpenters often have strips left over. You just have to keep your eyes open. "Quick, Henry, stop the car. I saw something back there." Or, if you have a table saw, it's easy enough to cut strips of wood yourself. The wood or blind grids can be painted, which kids love to do, creating fancy combinations of colors. For the best visual effect, I think plain white is best. (Kids will say, "Blah!") You can also write on them. (Kids will say, "Cool!") Some people like to record what they've planted. It's fun to have visitors sign your grid, especially children and grandchildren. Let them pick out which square they like best, and tell them it can be theirs. When they call, you can tell them how their plants are doing. I bet they'll call more often.

Protecting Your SFG

To protect one or more squares next to each other from weather or pests, the first step is to make a wire U-frame cage to fit over those squares. You may want to make several U-frames of different sizes that can be used for 1, 2, or 4 square feet and another for an entire 4×4 block of 16 square feet. Basically, you want to make a wire cage that will fit over the top of each of these areas. Later you can attach a covering made from any number of materials to protect those squares from a variety of hazards. I've found that the easiest cage is made from plastic-coated wire fencing. This can be cut with wire

To build a protective cage for your 4×4 garden, you'll need: four one inch by two inch boards, 4 feet long; chicken wire; plastic ties; cutting shears; and a power drill.

Arrange your boards as shown in this photo and drill two holes in one end of each board.

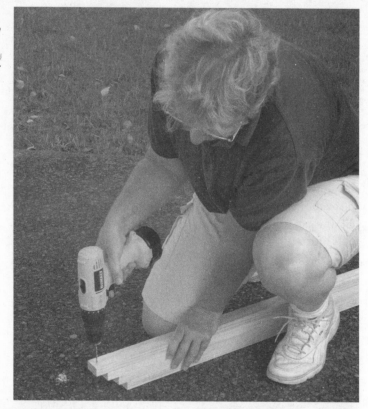

Attach the boards with two coarse-thread deck screws using your power drill.

pliers and easily bent over a straight edge to almost any shape. You can make a four-sided wire box from two U-frames or just a two-sided one. There is quite a variety of fencing wire to choose from so check out what is available. It comes in rolls of different widths and lengths as well as different openings and wire thicknesses. You may want to call ahead to several places to find the best choice.

Chicken Wire

Another common material I like to use is chicken wire. It comes in smaller 1-inch openings or larger 2-inch openings. The 1-inch size is much stronger but will cost a little more. The 1-inch size also takes a little longer to bend into shape but will keep out more critters than the 2-inch size. Chicken wire can be cut with pliers or cutting shears. It's sharp, so be sure to wear gloves. You can buy a whole roll of it, 3 or 4 feet wide. In many hardware stores you can buy whatever length you want from their roll, and they will cut it for you!

Full Cage

A chicken wire cage over the entire 4×4 makes it fairly easy to protect your garden against unwanted rabbits, birds that dig up and eat newly planted seeds, cats that like to dig in the soil, too much sun on newly planted and delicate seedlings, or strong wind gusts during the windy season. Build your wire cage to fit the plants' mature sizes. (Once plants start growing through the wire, it is very difficult to

Roll out one long piece of chicken wire and place your frame close to the center. Bracing the frame with your foot, bend the chicken wire up. Then, do this again for the other side. Remember to wear gloves!

take the cage off.) Grab the cage wire with your fingers and lift the whole thing off, tend to the plants, and then put it back down. A full cage needs a wooden-frame bottom for support, but it then fits nicely on your wooden garden box frame. See how everything in SFG fits together so nicely, just like Legos.

Construction

To make a wooden bottom for a wire cage, attach four pieces of 1×2 inch pine lumber 4 feet long in a box shape with two deck screws at each corner. Then cut and shape your chicken wire or fencing wire to the 4×4 box to create any height you want. Staple the wire to the wood frame using 3/8-inch staples, and then wire or tie the vertical corners together or wherever the wire forms a corner. If you are using chicken wire or any wire that has sharp edges, you may want to cover the sharp points—including where the wire is stapled to the wood—with something like duct tape (choose a nice color) to prevent getting scratched while you're moving your cover. Another way is to attach the wire to the inside of the 1×2 frame. It's a little more work to staple the wire to the inside, but there won't be any sharp points to scratch you. If you have a couple of these cages made up ahead of time—one or two that are 6 inches tall, another couple

Brace the frame with your foot and bend the chicken wire up.

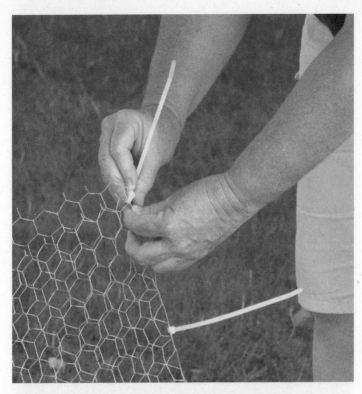

Once the wire is bent on all sides, remove the wood frame and connect the four corners at three locations using the plastic ties.

Set your wire frame over the wood frame and connect the wire with the plastic ties. Use the ties at random points on top of the frame, too.

The frame is light-weight and is easy to lift off your 4 × 4. Remove it to water, plant, prune, or harvest.

When placing your protective cage, make sure the frames line up. This will keep all kinds of critters from taking your harvest.

12 inches tall, and a few at 18 inches tall—they will be available at the right time they're needed for your garden. Don't forget you can use them as a framework for spring protection from cold, cats, or crows. They can be summer protection from sun, wind, and rain, and fall protection from deer, frosts, and snow. They can be stacked on the ground in a pile or hung on the garage or fence wall.

Covers

Materials used for covering the wire cages can be anything from clear plastic to protect plants from wind or cold weather and snow, sleet, or rain—to some sort of cloth like cheesecloth or floating cover to protect plants from insects getting in to lay their eggs.

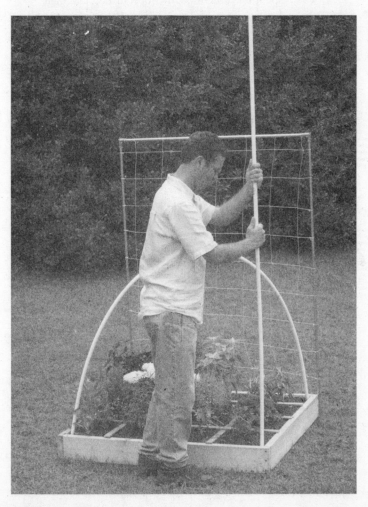

Bend two 10-foot PVC pipes of ¹/₂-inch diameter from corner to corner.

Clothespins

A cover can be easily held in place with clothespins. The cover can be open on some sides to allow air to circulate or it can be completely enclosed. One consideration, of course, is whether too much heat will build up inside the cage, and that depends on the season and the amount of sunlight your garden receives in your area. When there is too much sunlight for newly planted transplants, just put a shade cloth over the top of your cage. If you have several newly planted squares among other well-established plant squares, you can attach shade patches over just those plants that need a little shade.

Protective Dome Supports

A dome support is so easy to make. Just bend a 10-foot length of ½-inch PVC pipe from corner to corner of your box, and then another from the opposite corners; then tie or bolt it at the intersection at the top to make a dome that can support any type of cover. Think of it as the structural framework for a greenhouse—in the early spring it can be covered with clear plastic, in the late spring with cheesecloth to keep out egg-laying insects, and in the summer with shade cloth to provide a little shade for tender young plants. You can provide protection the same way for the fall crop.

Your two pipes should make a dome as shown here.

Attach a plastic tie at the intersection to ensure that it doesn't fall over.

Use a thick plastic cover to protect your plants from frost. Place some heavy objects such as bricks on the edges to secure it.

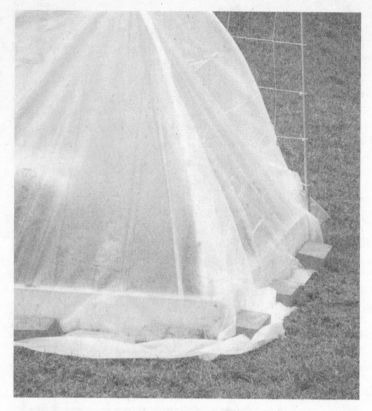

Covered Wagon

Another neat looking PVC frame is one in the shape of a covered wagon. This takes a little longer to make and requires just a bit more material, but it gives a lot more room and is much easier to use when you have a cover over the frame. It requires the same two 10-foot long PVC pipes, but they're arched over each end of your box. Then, you need an extra 4-foot-long piece of pipe that becomes the strut holding the two arches from collapsing. Tying the intersection will not work in this design, so you have to drill holes in the center of the arches and in each end of the strut, so that a bolt will connect the central strut to the top center of each arch. Use a bolt and nut that won't tear the plastic or net covering. Now you can see the shape is much more conducive to lifting one side to work inside, and it makes it easier to throw a blanket over the entire 4×4 on a cold night.

For those that don't want such a high frame, you just cut the 10-foot PCV pipes down to 6 or 8 feet and you'll have a much lower wagon top. For those of you thinking, "I'll just buy one 10-footer and cut it in half," that won't work. The arch over a 4-foot span has to be more than 5 feet long.

Locate the center of your two ten-foot pipes.

Drill one hole in the center of two 10-foot PVC pipes.

Place each pipe in a corner and bend as shown.

Drill holes in the ends of a 4-foot PVC pipe. It will be the supporting strut. Insert a plastic cable tie through the holes or a nut and a bolt to keep it in place.

Plant Supports

What do you do with heavy fruiting plants such as peppers, eggplants, and giant marigolds? The easiest way to support the branches of these plants without doing a lot of staking and tying is to make a permanent cage that the plants can grow through. The cage's height depends on the height of the mature plants. This could be for 1 square foot, 2, 4, or for the whole 16 square feet in a 4×4 garden; it all depends on what is planted in each square. The cage can be self-supporting with sides that stick into the soil just like the wire U-frame previously mentioned, or, if you are making a support for the entire 4×4, it is very easy to put a stake of some sort in each corner—either wood or metal—and then suspend the wire horizontally between these four corners.

Even better, if you are supporting the entire 4×4-foot area, put in the four corner stakes and then horizontally tie on some nylon tomato trellis netting. This netting is available at most garden stores and is particularly good because it is soft and cushiony and won't cut the plants when they rub against it in the wind. It also has large openings you can reach in to and the plants can grow through. It won't bother any of the shorter plants either. It is very easy material to work with and well-suited for gardening. Corner posts must be very strong and firmly held so the horizontal wire or netting won't sag. Posts can be constructed of wood and driven into the ground or attached with deck screws to the inside or outside corner of the wood frame. You can also use PVC pipe or even metal pipe or fence posts. The many options available show how flexible Square Foot Gardening can be.

Hold Me Up

Tall lanky plants such as dahlias, gladiolas, and sunflowers may also need extra support as they mature and grow in height. Sunflower seeds will need temporary protection when first planted to prevent birds or rabbits from digging up the seeds and to prevent other birds from eating the young sprouts. Temporarily covering your garden with chicken wire 6 inches over the box will provide this protection until the plants get that tall. Then, after the plants reach a height of about 3 feet, it is time to put in four corner posts—strong steel fence posts and nylon netting horizontally at several different levels. Start the first at 3 feet and the last should be as high as the fence posts. This will support plants through to maturity and keep them from falling over in heavy wind and rainstorms.

Corn Protection

Everyone loves corn—especially chipmunks, squirrels, and raccoons! To keep them out and your harvest in, try this foolproof secret. Put one steel fence post in each corner of your 4×4 foot garden. Use tall metal 5- or 6-foot fence posts, and then, when corn reaches 4 feet, run chicken wire with 1-inch openings around the outside forming four walls. Next, add one more piece across the top at a height of about 4 feet. This will keep the critters out of the corn and prevent the crows from eating the seeds and seedlings when first planted. Then, as the corn grows, it will grow right through the top of the wire, which will support the tall corn stalks when the wind blows—at the same time, keeping the raccoons and chipmunks out before the corn can be harvested. You can easily tie the horizontal top wire with temporary bows so that you can undo a few and still reach in. Since it is chicken wire, make sure you wear a long-sleeved shirt when you reach in so you don't get scratched. You'll be able to water easily either by hand or using a long-handled wand and shut-off valve on the end of your hose.

> *"SFG is great for the family. Each person has his or her own plot."*
> —Gary from Michigan

Vertical Frames for Vine Crops

When I first invented the Square Foot Gardening method, I knew one of the real challenges was going to be some of the big sprawling vine crops like tomatoes. Without a doubt, tomatoes are America's most-loved garden vegetable. However, they can take up a lot of room and can become unsightly by season's end if they are allowed to grow without proper care. Also, if left to sprawl over the ground, tomatoes can attract additional pests, and many get damaged or ruined from foot traffic. The whole idea of growing tomatoes this way seemed very non-productive.

I was determined to find a better way to grow tomatoes and what I devised turned out to be not only good for tomatoes, but for all other vine crops too. Every plant that has a vine that sprawls all over the ground—even pumpkins and watermelons—can be grown vertically as long as you have a strong enough support; the result is a spectacular sight with very little wasted ground space.

Air Rights

Being an engineer, I thought of buildings in a city. Buildings aren't constructed as one-story structures that sprawl outward over the landscape; space is too valuable to do this. Instead, designers and contractors use what is called air rights, building straight up into the air, floor after floor after floor. Why can't plants be grown the same way? Well, I discovered they can! All you need is a strong framework and something to hold the vine onto the framework. Did you know that vines grow better vertically than horizontally? Growing plants vertically prevents ground rot and discourages pest infestation. I know slugs aren't happy about my way of vertical gardening; I hear they get dizzy up high, but that's their problem!

Nature Supports

Through the years I experimented with all different types of materials and frames. Finally, I settled upon one that was so simple, easy, and inexpensive to use that it was almost ridiculous. Then I began growing all different types of plants vertically. I originally thought I would need to design some special way to hold up and accommodate heavier fruits such as winter squash and pumpkins, but as it turned out, these plant vines seemed to understand the situation; the stem supporting the heavy fruit grows thicker and heavier as the fruit becomes larger. If you have a framework and support that will hold the plant, the plant will hold the fruit; it is as simple as that! Mother Nature always seems to know best.

✓ **SHOPPING LIST**

- Steel reinforcing rods
- Steel pipes (electrical conduit)
- Connectors
- Nylon netting

Best Material

I use the strongest material I can find, which is steel. Fortunately, steel comes in tubular pipe used for electrical conduit. It is very strong and turns out to be very inexpensive. Couplings are also available so you can connect two pieces together. I designed an attractive frame that fits right onto the 4×4 box, and it can be attached to the wooden box with clamps that can be bought at any store. Or, steel reinforcing rods driven into the existing ground outside your box provide a very steady and strong base; then the electrical conduit slips snugly over the bars. It's very simple and inexpensive to assemble. Anyone can do it—even you! To prevent vertically grown plants from shading other parts of the garden, I recommend that tall, vertical frames be constructed on the north side of the garden. To fit it into a 4×4 box, I designed a frame that measured 4 feet wide and almost 6 feet tall.

Tie It Tight

Vertically growing plants need to be tied to their supports. Nylon netting won't rot in the sun and weather, and I use it exclusively now for both vertical frames and horizontal plant supports. It is very strong— almost unbreakable—and guaranteed for twenty years. It is a wonderful material available at garden stores and in catalogs. The nylon netting is also durable enough to grow the heavier vine crops on vertical frames, including watermelons, pumpkins, cantaloupes, winter and summer squashes, and tomatoes. You will see in Chapter 8 how easy it is to train plants to grow vertically. To hold the plants to the frame, I have found that nylon netting with 7-inch square openings made especially for tomato growing works well because you can reach your hand through. Make sure it is this type so it won't cut the stem of the plant when it blows against it in the wind. This comes in 4-foot widths and can easily be tied to the metal frame. It's sometimes hard to find, so call around.

Winter Storage

Because the netting is loose, it can flop around unless you tie it very tightly to the frame; this is the first step. At the end of the season the frames can be left up or they can be slipped off the steel rebar and hung on a garage wall. Although the conduit is galvanized and endures many years of service, it eventually will rust—especially at the bottom where it comes in contact with the ground. If you do hang up your metal frames in the winter, for safety reasons make sure you cover or clearly mark the steel rebar that is left sticking out of the ground. You can flag it with brightly covered tape, paint it, or find caps that can be screwed on to prevent someone from tripping.

Composters

A composting operation can be as simple as a pile of leaves, weeds, and kitchen scraps. Mother Nature does it all the time. Go to any forest or field and you'll see she gets the job done without any structures. But people are different. We like to conserve space, keep things in their place; and we usually want to build a container or enclosure for our compost materials, which speeds up the operation by creating bulk, which then allows the pile to heat up and decompose faster.

What can we buy or build? There are many compost containers on the market mostly made from plastic. All work well, are attractive, and reasonably priced. There are composters that tumble or turn, speeding up the process, but they cost more and worst of all—**you** still have to turn them. It's fun at first but it gets old very fast.

Make Your Own

We need a structure that will hold a pile of material in either a round or square shape. Wire fencing works well for round and even square structures if you use four fence posts. Make wire cylinders at least 3 to 4 feet in diameter. The exact length of fencing you'll need isn't critical. Instead I am just going to tell everyone to buy 10 or 15 feet of fencing and shape it in a cylinder by attaching the ends together by bending the cut wire ends.

So, if you want a 3-foot diameter composter, buy 10 feet of fenc- *If you don't have a*
ing. If you want a 4-foot diameter, buy 15 feet of fencing and have *compost pile yet, start*
enough for a door. And, if you don't like round composters, buy four *one now. It's essential*
6-foot long steel fence posts, drive them in each corner of your com- *to the Square Foot*
poster location, bend the wire around those, and you'll have a square *Gardening method.*
composter, much more suited to SFG. Find the best location for your
composter and fill as explained in Chapter 5. When full or ready to
turn, just lift up the wire cylinder, place it next to the pile, and use a
garden fork to fill the cylinder in its new location—you've just turned
the pile!

With a Gate

Another idea is to have an enclosure that's easier to get into to mix and
water or even turn. Make an entrance opening with or without a gate.
Start by driving two steel fence posts in the ground at your selected location; make them about 3 or 4 feet apart. Then attach your wire fencing
to these posts. Two options are available for you—with and without a
gate. If you want a gate it will cost you an extra 3 or 4 feet of fencing.
No big deal, and it will look nicer and be neater when the enclosure
starts filling up. You still tie or wire the fencing to both fence posts; one
becomes the hinge, the other the door latch.

Make the latch S-hook from wire, or you can buy this type of
hook at the store. You can have one compost bin or two together or
even three depending on how large your operation is.

Weekly Bins

Just like the wire enclosures, you can have one, two, or up to six bins all together for Monday through Saturday. (Don't forget we rest on Sunday!) When and why would you need more than one? When you get serious about composting, you may be able to get enough material to fill up one every week. Then, for mixing (as explained in Chapter 5), you just move material from a full bin into an empty one right next to it. The nice thing about a series is you only need three pallets for each additional bin.

I could include directions for other materials to use like bricks or cement blocks, landscape timbers, or logs, but no one is going to build a composter out of those materials. They would be too expensive and inefficient. They may look good in books but not in our system because they are just not practical.

Of course, no one says you have to have an enclosure, but if you're a Square Foot Gardener and you have nice square boxes for all of your garden, why would you want just a pile for your composter?

PENNY PINCHER

SQUARE IS GOOD

Here's a no-cost easy way to make your composter out of wood—that means free. Women tell me they love this because it requires no tools, wire cutting, equipment, or familiarity with construction. Find four wood pallets of similar size and appearance. You can find discarded pallets everywhere. The place to find them is behind the stores and shops where the dumpsters are. Ask first, just to make sure they are being thrown out. If you can fine four of about the same size and look, your finished composter will look like it's custom made just for you. A brick or stone under each corner helps keep the wood off the ground to keep it from rotting; corners are tied with rope, cord, or chain. It doesn't have to be nailed or screwed together, and it doesn't have to be real tight. You may want to have the pallet boards face outside to look nice, and you can make them all run either horizontally or vertically—whatever looks best.

Aisles

"Put your best foot forward" is the saying, but what are you going to put it on? Grass, brick, boards, gravel, or just plain dirt? Most people put their Square Foot boxes in their yard and leave the grass for their aisles. This helps keep a natural look. And don't worry, the grass won't get a lot of hard use because there's not that much to do in a Square Foot Garden. If you want to leave natural soil in your aisles use an action hoe once a week to rid your aisle of pesky weeds.

Brick Paths

In my PBS TV garden, we had a small 15 × 15 area with several boxes and plain dirt aisles. I spent five minutes every week running an action hoe over the soil to cut off any new weeds, and it looked pretty nice. But then in one of the classes I was giving, some of the ladies wanted to know how to lay brick so I thought this would be fun to teach as well as improving the garden. So without moving the boxes, we laid down many layers of newspaper. Next we added a 1-inch layer

MEL SAYS...

If you don't want grass in your aisles, lay down a mulch. Here again, you want to first dig out any weeds or grass; then to prevent weeds from growing back without using chemicals, you can put down a landscape fabric or weed cloth. There are many on the market today. They come in 3- or 4-foot wide rolls and do quite a good job. (Don't use regular black plastic—it won't drain and it's slippery.) Then just cover the cloth with at least 1 or 2 inches of mulch.

You can also use gravel, which comes in all different kinds and sizes, colors and shapes, or you can use other types of ground cover like ground up bark or pine needles; I've even seen people use straw, hay, salt hay, or even leaves collected and saved from last fall. As you walk, these materials break up and gradually decompose, creating something you can add later to your compost pile.

You can also build walkways out of brick, wood planks, or paving stones. Again, take out any weeds and put down a weed cloth first. You can create some very interesting patterns with bricks and paving blocks. Keep the joints fairly tight so the surface doesn't shift.

Go to the nursery department of your local home improvement center and browse through it to find the ground cover material you prefer.

of sand and then started laying bricks right on that sand base. No mortar or cement is needed—just fill in the tight joints with loose sand. When we got to the existing 4×4 garden boxes, we just went right around them. It went well and in one afternoon it was all done. What an improvement—wow! We added some patio furniture, and this area became a favorite spot to sit and enjoy the yard and gardens. We also began to notice more of a different kind of visitor to the garden—the birds and bees and butterflies and so many more insects. And all for the price of a few bricks (well, a small truckload actually) and a little sand.

One Last Idea

How would you like to carpet your garden . . . wall to wall? Well, you can. Buy new or used indoor/outdoor patio carpeting. It even comes in a grass style but, don't worry, you won't have to mow it!

Let's Review

When building a SFG, start with the basic building block—a 4×4 bottomless wood box. Then, depending on the situation, add special features to solve any gardening problem or to protect your garden from any hazard. Some of the simple additions you can add to your SFG boxes:

- A wire bottom to keep out moles, voles, and gophers
- A weed cloth bottom to keep out weeds or grass
- A chicken wire top to keep out cats, dogs, and rabbits
- A PVC top frame then:
  - Clear plastic to create a miniature greenhouse
  - Bird or deer netting
  - A blanket to protect plants from frosts
  - Floating covers to protect from insects
- The possibilities are endless for everyone, from apartment dwellers to the elderly, and even people with special needs.

After all this talk about building all these different things for protecting your garden, I don't want you to become worried, thinking that you have to spend a lot of time creating complex structures

PENNY PINCHER

Kill Weeds for Free

Some gardeners use indoor or outdoor carpeting either face up, or if you don't like the color or texture, face down. This is a good way to smother and kill grass or weeds in the aisles without any digging. However, once it rains, indoor carpet gets soggy and smelly, so out it goes.

Where do you get old carpet? Go to your local carpet store; they have tons of it out by the dumpster. Don't ask them to deliver it though. If it's new stuff you are going to buy, they may deliver that free once you buy it. They'll even cut it for you to the width of your aisles.

for your SFG. It's not so! We've just learned how easy it is to adjust a SFG to improve its flexibility and to accommodate unique gardening situations. This is readily done since a SFG is so small and manageable. For the most part, your plants will just sit there quietly growing, looking better and better every day. So relax and enjoy!

Family

But remember, protecting your garden is a lot like protecting your children—if it's cold, add a blanket (a sweater); if sleet and hail are predicted, add clear plastic (a raincoat); and if it's windy, add an extra shield against the wind (a windbreaker). Since you wouldn't let your kids play out in the cold winter without a snowsuit for protection, do the same for your plants. Keeping this in mind, you'll be able to come up with easy and practical solutions for protecting your garden from the worst of conditions. That makes it very rewarding because then you can enjoy your garden much longer every year.

This simple PVC frame can protect your plants from many things including harmful weather and unwanted nibblers. (I'm not talking about you!)

Mel's Mix, Essential for Square Foot Gardening Success

Mel's Mix

Mel's Mix is the most important, productive, essential, necessary, critical, major subject and is the backbone of the entire book and the Square Foot Gardening method!

That's the picture. Get it? It is the reason all the other improvements are possible. So, please, pay attention, study, and learn everything in this chapter so you can make your Mel's Mix the best you can. This will allow you to automatically have all the other benefits and improvements that come so naturally to (the all new) SFG.

Don't Skimp On This

Now, with All New Square Foot Gardening you'll never have to do all the hard work, expense, and time-consuming, back-breaking labor of improving your garden soil every spring like we used to do. Your Mel's Mix is ready to go whenever you are. It never has to be replaced and you don't have to do a thing except plant your seeds.

Mel's Mix may be the most costly part of SFG, yet at the same time it is the most cost effective. How can it be both? The answer: if you try to skimp on this item, you'll be disappointed in all the rest. But, if you do it right, all the other advantages of SFG will fall into place and you will be the richest gardener on the block. Sorry to be so adamant, but this is really what makes SFG so different and successful. We have never had a failure of SFG except when someone decided to skimp on the ingredients to save a few bucks.

Let's review what this perfect soil will do for your garden, then the why and how so you fully understand the nature of the mix.

We'll go through each of the three ingredients indicated—compost, peat moss, and vermiculite—and what each one is, why you need it, and where to obtain it all. Then I'll discuss how to mix, moisten, and place it in your boxes. If you do it right, you'll have the most enjoyable gardening experience of your life. That wonderful feeling will be repeated every time you plant and replant every single square foot. Your hand will just slip through the loose, easily worked, earthy-smelling soil, and you will sigh with happiness and smile every time. It is truly an emotional experience that very few gardeners have ever encountered. But enough talk and teasing—let's get started!

THINGS YOU HAVE TO KNOW

Backyard Soil For Single Row Gardening:

Structure	pH
Drainage	Fertilizer
Texture	Blending
Organic content	

Mel's Mix For Square Foot Gardening:
  The Formula

No More

This is a partial list of just some of the knowledge you had to learn about backyard soils in the past. But not now! Forget about every one of them. Why? Because Square Foot Gardening is now so simple you don't have to learn all the intricate details of soil structure, texture, and drainage. You don't even have to know what pH means, how to pronounce it, or which letter is a capital and which is lower case (or why people are always getting that mixed up). Why, you may ask? Because I've designed our perfect soil mix with the correct pH level (acid or alkaline) for just about all plants.

For those of you who crave more information, a good, blended, balanced compost—one of the ingredients in Mel's Mix and what you will add to your boxes after each harvest—made from at least five different ingredients will not only have a pH close to neutral, but it also balances the acidity in peat moss. In addition, since we don't use your existing soil (remember we only need 6 inches of pure Mel's Mix), you won't be concerned with what type of soil it is or what the pH is. You won't have to buy a pH soil test kit or take samples to your county extension agent. You won't have to learn that eastern U.S.A. soils are slightly acidic while western soils are more alkaline, and you won't have to learn what to add, how much, and when. You won't have to buy a spreader or any of that stuff.

No Fertilizer, No Mess

Mel's Mix has all the nutrients, minerals, and trace elements that plants need. So forget all about fertilizer. Isn't that amazing? Not only do you not have to buy it, you don't even have to learn about it. SFG is an all-organic, all-natural method.

Come spring you'll find there is no work to do; there is no going to the store, reading labels, lugging big bags or bales of soil additives home, no spreading them out, working in lime, getting a rototiller running and working—then trying to turn over that wet, mucky soil, getting it all over your shoes and tools—oh, what a mess that was. But that is all a thing of the past. Why, you don't even have to do the soilball test in the palm of your hand only to find out you have to wait another week because your soil is too wet or still frozen. (What's the soilball test, you ask? I'm not going to tell you because you don't need to know it any longer.)

Your Mel's Mix is always ready to plant no matter what the weather. It's always loose, friable (which the experts define as that which is easily worked—good and crumbly), and ready for the right time of year to plant. It drains and becomes unfrozen so much quicker than regular garden soil.

Where Have You Been?

Planting a garden will no longer depend on when the soil is ready but only on the right date to plant seeds and transplants. This is just one more simplification of gardening the Square Foot way. How does that all sound? Simple and easy—no work, no muss, no fuss. I have had people ask me, "Why weren't you born one hundred years ago so I could have started with Square Foot Gardening instead of having to do all the work of single-row gardening all my life?" Good question!

No Digging

Using Mel's Mix completely eliminates all the hard work of digging and moving existing soil. A 4×4×12-inch-deep area contains 16 cubic feet of soil that weighs well over 400 pounds. That's a lot of soil to dig up and move around. All gardening in the past has been based upon improving your existing soil. My original book had rather complicated instructions for your soil, but we've changed all that. Don't even be concerned about it. You don't have to know anything about soils. Just start with a perfect growing soil—Mel's Mix of 1/3 compost, 1/3 peat moss, and 1/3 vermiculite measured by volume.

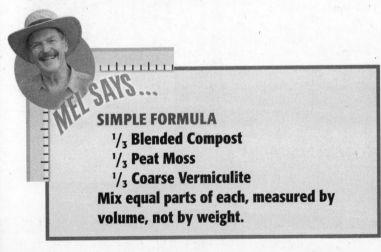

MEL SAYS...

SIMPLE FORMULA
   1/3 Blended Compost
   1/3 Peat Moss
   1/3 Coarse Vermiculite
Mix equal parts of each, measured by volume, not by weight.

Like A Sponge

Through many experiments, I came up with the very best ingredients for that perfect growing soil. Of course, I made sure they were all inexpensive, readily available, and able to hold just the right amount of moisture for plants while not becoming too soggy for roots, which might drown your plants. I created a formula that holds moisture yet drains well.

At first this seemed like an impossible task, but then I thought about sponges. When you take a dry sponge and slowly add water to it, it just keeps soaking up water until it's finally saturated. At that point, any extra water just drains out the bottom. Well, it turns out that two of our ingredients—peat moss and vermiculite—do exactly that same thing. It takes a while to wet them and keep them moist so you have to keep adding water, but finally, when they become saturated, any excess water just drains right out the bottom. Peat moss and vermiculite are sold at garden nurseries, home improvement centers, and even some grocery stores.

Three ingredients make up Mel's Mix: Peat moss, vermiculite, and blended compost. Combined properly, Mel's Mix retains moisture, drains perfectly, and has all the nutrients and trace minerals a plant could ever want.

LEFT: *An assortment of composts is shown here. You'll need at least 5 different types of compost for Mel's Mix. Pay no attention to weight; go by the volume, even if you have to estimate it.*

MIDDLE: *Buying peat moss in 3.9 cubic foot bales is the most cost-efficient. The smaller bags of loose peat moss are more expensive. The same goes for vermiculite; ask for the large 4.0 cubic foot size. Don't settle for the small bags measured by quarts.*

BELOW: *Make a neat cut in the top of your bags. This way, when you've finished making your own Mel's Mix, you can reuse the bags to store any leftover mix.*

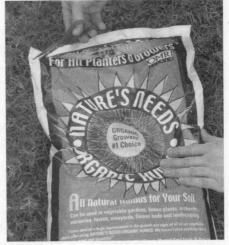

Important Note: *If volume is not marked on the bags, compare them to similarly sized bags where volume is marked to estimate.*

Math 101

The biggest problem turns out to be arithmetic, not the materials. All three ingredients in Mel's Mix are sold in different-sized bags or bales, and this may make it harder to figure out how much of each you need. But, don't worry, I'm going to give you some examples so you won't even have to think about the math.

1 Compost

Let's take a minute to describe compost. It is one-third of the Mel's Mix, and it is also what you add to your All New Square Foot Garden after you harvest each square foot. So what is it, how do you make it, and why bother?

Compost is absolutely the best material in which to grow your plants. Good compost has all the nutrients needed for plant growth. It's loose and friable and easily worked. It holds lots of moisture yet drains well. It's easy to make yet hard to find. The best kind is homemade compost that you make in your own backyard. The worst kind is the single ingredient byproduct some company has produced and bagged.

Good and Bad

So, let's simplify garden composting and garden compost.

First off, it's a very confusing subject because the word "compost" is both a noun and a verb. As a noun, compost is described as a rich, crumbly, soil-like material used in gardening. As a verb, it is the process of breaking down plant material that is no longer growing through a decomposition process.

To complicate the understanding of the garden-related, breaking-down process (compost as a verb), there are actually two types of processes—aerobic, with air; and anaerobic, without air. Both are a natural, Mother Earth process. But the first, or aerobic, has no odor, heats up, and does its job with little microbes wearing white hats (the good guys). The second, or anaerobic process, smells, is messy, and is very objectionable. The more common name for this is rotting. I don't have to tell you that all these microbe bugs wear black hats (the bad guys). It's true all those bad-guy, black-hat items will eventually decompose, but you don't want to be around while they do.

What to Use

Any plant material is perfect for adding to your compost pile as long as it's not hosting a plant disease or pest. When the ingredients are all piled together and if they have enough bulk, they will decompose organically by the aerobic process all by themselves. But it takes time; Mother Nature can't be hurried. Some people say, "I can't wait for a year or two. How can I speed this process?" **The answer—mix, mash, moisten, and move.**

QUICK COMPOST

Keep everything moist, make a big pile, and keep turning it. How often? Every day if you want the finished compost in two weeks; every week for results in three months; or every month for it to be ready in a year. The ideal conditions for the fastest results are:

1. **Mix—add as many different, plant-based ingredients as you can find.**
2. **Mash—chop everything up into small pieces.**
3. **Moisten—not dry or wet, just moist.**
4. **Move—keep turning the pile towards the center where all the action is.**

The results will be the most amazing material you could hope for in your garden. It's often called black gold because of the color of the finished product called compost.

Needs Mass

Using the right ingredients and mixing, mashing, moistening, and moving them will help speed the composting. But there is one more ideal condition, and that is mass. The more bulk you have in your pile (up to a certain point), the faster it will compost or decompose. If your pile is taller than 4 feet, you'll have a hard time adding new ingredients. If the area is larger than 4×4, the air will have trouble getting into the center where all the action is and the white-hat, good-guy microbes will turn into the black-hat, bad-guy microbes and the pile will start to decompose anaerobically (without air) and start to smell. If you don't have enough bulk—smaller than 3×3, your pile will just sit there and do nothing except cry out, "I'm going to wait for Mother Nature."

We keep calling it a pile, and you may wonder if it will be ugly and messy. But the pile can be contained very nicely with a homemade or store-bought container called a composter. (Oh no! Another name!) So now, I'm going to be **composting** my **compost** in my **composter**. You've got it! See, that wasn't so bad.

Still Confused?

Way back when I wrote my first book on SFG, I had no idea people would be so confused about composting until I realized that only 10 percent of gardeners actually compost, another 10 percent don't ever want to compost, and the middle 80 percent say they would like to but are confused and scared by the process. Of course, much of that confusion is from not knowing how to compost aerobically.

Let's summarize.

✓ TIPS FOR SUCCESSFUL COMPOSTING

	Yes	No
Ingredients	Once growing plants	Animal parts
	Made from plant	Manmade with
	material	synthetic parts
Necessary Size	Between 3x3x3 to	Under 3x3x3 or larger
	4x4x4 feet	than 4x4x4
Moisture	Moist	Too dry or too wet
Mixing	As often as	Never
	you can	

Compost Ingredients

What you need to remember about the ingredients is that animal byproducts are not good for your compost. Eggshells are okay; just crush and sprinkle around. Manure is okay from plant-eating animals, but no manure from meat-eating animals.

Turn the Handles or Chop, Chop, Chop

If you are in a real hurry, there are expensive, but effective, rotating drum composters you can buy. You just turn a handle, flip a container, or push a barrel around, and the contents are mixed and moved. Great idea, and they work if you do it regularly.

I've also heard of, but never tried, the closed, black-plastic-bag-of-ingredients-left-in-the-garage-over-the-winter method. Be careful when you open the bag because, as you can guess, that method uses the black-hat, no air, anaerobic process that smells.

Some gardeners have tried using plastic or molded garbage cans or even larger trash containers. You have to drill or poke holes in them so the air can get in, but if the lid is tight-fitting, you could roll it around every day.

On my PBS TV program, I showed how to make a rolling composter out of an old, cleaned oil drum. You could push it with your foot to roll it around. It was great.

I've found from my own experimenting that, no matter what method you use, the sooner you mix and move and the more you mash (cut or chop), the sooner and faster you'll start the composting action going. Just add compost ingredients by mixing it in with the top of the existing pile. Each time you add a lot or just a little, stir it into the top of the pile and mix it in well. But, don't just add it in layers.

Practical Composting Tips

Mow Those Leaves

Save some of your leaves from fall to add to the compost pile next year rather than all at once. After you rake them up, run the lawnmower over them to chop them up and then stuff into plastic bags (make sure they are dry) or, if you are a "neatnik," store them in gray garbage bins stored along the wall of your compost operation.

Dry That Grass

Others like to save their grass clippings the same way, but you have to be very careful. If piled up, fresh green grass will quickly turn into a

DETAILED LIST OF INGREDIENTS

Yes Each item should be under 20 percent of total by volume	Caution – Limited Amounts Each item should be under 10 percent of total	No 0 percent
Straw	Corn cobs	Diseased or pest-laden materials
Hay (including salt hay)	Shredded twigs	Meat or bones
Leaves	Shredded bark	Grease
Grass clippings (dried)	Pine needles	Whole eggs
Old sod	Hedge trimmings	Cheese
Reject or spoiled garden produce	Wood shavings	Seeds and fruit pits
Vegetable and fruit peels	Sawdust	Cat or dog manure
Newspaper (shredded)	Coffee grounds	Bakery products
Eggshells (crushed)	Peanut shells	Dairy products
Stable or poultry manure		Supper plate scrapings or
Tea bags		kitchen scraps

black-hat, anaerobic operation that's a stinking, slimy, gooey mess. Grass clippings have to be dried before adding them to the pile or stored for later addition. It does seem like an oxymoron to dry the grass clippings only to moisten them in the compost pile, but now I'm sure you can see why we do it that way.

I compare it to my mother's meatloaf. She would dry bread and then crumble it to make bread crumbs. She would then add milk to moisten everything. If she had just added moist, fresh bread, it would have gotten clumpy and gooey. The compost is similar. If material is put in wet, it packs down in clumps preventing air from entering the pile, and then it rots and smells.

So spread your grass clippings out on a tarp or the driveway, turn them a few times with a rake or flip your tarp before storing them or adding them to your compost pile. How long? Until the grass is brownish and dry to the touch. It depends on the sun, humidity, and rain, as well as the climate of your location.

Mix and Turn

This is a good time to remind you that the center of the pile is where most of the action is. It will be the hottest (up to 150° F or 65° C), the moistest, and with the most white-hats running around decomposing the ingredients. Knowing all that when you turn the contents of one compost bin into another, you will be putting the top of A into the bottom of B—assuming you have two bins or piles side-by-side—then you make sure you put the outside material of A into the inside of B. Get it? It's just like the theory that opposites attract.

Mix in (at the same time) opposite colors, wetness, size—everything opposite for the fastest operation. In other words, brown with green, wet with dry, coarse with fine. That's all easy to remember—just think of opposites attracting and you'll have a great operation.

If You Decide to Buy Compost

Don't buy all of one kind of compost if you decide to not make it yourself. Don't let the clerk sell you the "best and most popular," especially if it's loose and not bagged. Here's why. **All** commercial compost is a byproduct from one industry. It might be the wood, cattle, mushroom, cannery, cotton, or soybean industry that has a waste product and they have to get rid of it. They said, "What if we take our waste product (sawdust, manure, vines, pulp, or husks) and compost it, people will pay us and take it away." Everyone laughed but, by golly, it happened just that way. Now every industry with a waste product is finding ways to get rid of it at a profit all the while protecting the environment. What a good deal. The only setback for gardeners is most bags of compost come from a single product and have only one ingredient.

What's the solution? Buy a variety of composts and mix them together. Now, you are more likely to get a better mixture.

Go Big Time

If you are really into this, you can brainstorm to think of places that throw out organic or plant material. Like a bird shop and all those bird droppings that go on the bottom of the cage. And, how about the annual fire department community breakfast—fresh fruit, banana and orange peels maybe, but also how about eggshells? Just ask ahead—take boxes or bags and ask them to separate the trash. Or, how about the annual 4th of July watermelon picnic in town? There are all kinds of places where you can collect ingredients for your compost pile. And, you know, the nice thing is that you'll find the same situation the world over.

PENNY PINCHER

Your home operation should include every different thing you can think of. Go to the grocery store and ask for the produce manager. Many stores throw out tons of spoiled vegetables and fruits they can't sell. These are from all over the world, so just think of the different soils and climates all that has grown in and what different vitamins, minerals, and trace elements they contain. If they're not diseased, chop them up and mix them in the compost pile.

When I'm visiting foreign countries, my hosts say, "We are poor here, and we have nothing to compost." I take them on a tour and find all of these places have things that could be composted. It's always things people are throwing out. I've done that in India, Haiti, Argentina, Nepal, Thailand, Ghana, and even in London, Paris, Amsterdam, and New York City, so don't be afraid to go, look, and ask—it's out there.

PENNY PINCHER

COFFEE GROUNDS AND FREE BUCKETS

Anyplace people gather, there will be waste thrown out. Check out farmer's markets, local fairs or street carnivals, flea markets, even places like Starbucks (guess what they would have for you there?). In addition to compost material, many of these restaurant-type places have big buckets used for pickles, mayonnaise, or oil that make great water buckets— all free for the asking.

 Peat Moss

The second ingredient in Mel's Mix is peat moss. It's a natural material occurring on the earth that has been made after millions of years from decomposing plant material. You can usually determine how old peat moss is by measuring how deeply it's buried. It is commonly used in agriculture to improve existing soils because it makes them lighter, more friable, and water retentive.

There are plenty of debates about the use of peat moss because it's a nonrenewable resource. Because there is a limit to this valuable material I'd like to guide you in using it responsibly while maximizing its benefits.

Only a Little

The new SFG method uses only 20 percent of the space of traditional single-row gardens. Therefore, you automatically use only 20 percent—one-fifth— as much peat moss, an 80 percent reduction. In addition, with Square Foot Gardening, you add peat moss once and only once when you first create your Mel's Mix. Thereafter, you'll never need to add peat moss to the garden. (What you will add is compost, which is renewable.)

In the United States, most peat moss comes from the northern states and Canada where it is still readily available. Because it's such a valuable resource, SFG says let's not waste it. Instead let's get rid of all single-row gardens that require five times as much nonrenewable materials to improve the soil year after year. Let's be conservative and sensible and use what we have, a beneficial, natural material, but make it longer lasting.

 Vermiculite

Vermiculite, the third and final ingredient in Mel's Mix, is also a natural material and is obtainable all over the world. It's mica rock mined out of the ground. Once the rock is collected, it is then ground up into small particles and heated until it explodes just like popcorn, forming small pieces from as large as the tip of your little finger down to almost a powder. However, this material is filled with nooks and crannies, just like an English muffin. These nooks and crannies hold a tremendous amount of water and yet can breathe, making the soil extremely friable and loose. The moisture is always there for the roots to absorb. Remember that roots don't grow through soil; they grow around soil particles. That's why plants do better in a loose, friable soil because the roots have an easy time growing.

Certified

Vermiculite is graded into several sizes—fine, medium, and coarse—and is also tested and qualified for different types of uses. The coarse agricultural grade holds the most moisture while at the same time giving the most friability to the soil mix. You may find that some stores do not carry vermiculite. If you ask them why, you might hear a story that started many years ago when one mine in Montana was shut down because part of the mine was found to contain asbestos. Now, shutting down a mine because it contains asbestos makes sense.

However, some newspaper stories associated the problem with all of the products coming from the mine. Although the mine was shut down and the industry has produced a great deal of evidence that the contamination was not in the vermiculite, the story surfaces every few years as if it was new, thereby getting everyone upset all over again. It was a serious situation, but as a result, the good news is that all the vermiculite mines around the world and products sold are now meticulously inspected by everyone; the bags we buy now even come with a "Certified Asbestos Free" sticker.

Locating it can be difficult. Let your fingers do the walking and call around. Call all the major nurseries, garden supply centers, and major home improvement stores and try to get the garden manager on the phone and ask them if they carry the large 4-cubic-foot bags of coarse vermiculite because you're building a Square Foot Garden. If that fails, look under "greenhouse supplies or suppliers" in the yellow pages for wholesale distributors. Some people have found it at farm feed stores or even on the Internet.

There is one caution when you mix it, and it is the same caution with peat moss. Both materials are dusty when dry right out of the bag so wear gloves and a painting mask. Mix only outdoors on a calm day.

Perlite Instead of Vermiculite?

Perlite is another natural material mined out of the earth and used in agriculture for the same purpose as vermiculite—to break up and loosen poor soils and to retain moisture. I personally don't like or use perlite, and here's why. It is hard as a rock, rather coarse and gritty, and I don't like the feel of it in the soil mix. It doesn't hold moisture like vermiculite. In addition, it floats to the top of the soil mix as you water your garden and because it's white, it looks rather unsightly and unnatural. And it makes me sneeze! Many people do use perlite instead of vermiculite and, in fact, most of the commercial mixes are made with perlite because it's cheaper. It's a matter of preference and availability, but I know which one I'm buying.

Buying What You Need

If you found the math about area difficult in previous chapters, don't even bother with volume. Get the kids to do the math for you.

Why concern yourself with volume? Because you need to know the quantity of the three ingredients for Mel's Mix necessary to fill your boxes, and the packages for the different ingredients come in different sizes. But the good news is they usually use cubic feet as their measurement. If not, disregard weight and estimate by volume.

AREA X DEPTH EQUALS CUBIC FEET

Multiply the widths of your box, and divide it by 2 to figure out how much volume your six-inch-deep box will hold.

(4 × 4) / 2 = 8 cubic feet
(4 × 8) / 2 = 16 cubic feet
(4 × 12) / 2 = 24 cubic feet
(4 × 16) / 2 = 32 cubic feet

So, let's review how to figure volume. Volume is merely: area × depth=cubic feet. In other words, square feet (the area) times the depth equals cubic feet.

Our 4×4-foot box is 16 square feet in area (that's 4 feet times 4 feet). If it were 1 foot deep, the volume would be: 16 (the area) times 1 (the depth) equals 16 cubic feet. But it's not 1 foot deep, it's only 6 inches deep so we need only one-half or just 8 cubic feet for our 4×4 box. The math looks like this: 4 times 4 divided by one-half foot equals 8. Or to show it mathematically, (4×4)/2 = 8. (Now don't laugh, kids, some of the parents will be thankful for this kind of help).

Peat Moss (Compressed bale)

Full bale: 3.9 cubic feet compressed = 8 cubic feet loose
Half bale: 2.2 cubic feet compressed = 4 cubic feet loose
(These measurements aren't exact, but we're not mixing a cake here.)

Vermiculite (coarse)

Don't buy the small 4-quart sized or similar bag—insist on the 4-cubic-feet big bag. Call ahead to locate.

Mel's Mix Volume

Now here's the tricky part. Since all the products for Mel's Mix come in different volumes, you'll have to purchase them already knowing how much you'll need to mix correctly and fill your boxes completely. Let's use a hypothetical example. If we had 4×4 boxes, they would each have a volume of 8 cubic feet, as we determined already. So, if we had six boxes to fill, we would need 6×8 = 48 cubic feet of mix. (Six boxes times 8 cubic feet for each box equals 48 cubic feet of mix.) One-third of the total for each ingredient = 48/3 = 16 cubic feet of each. (A total of 48 cubic feet divided by three different ingredients equals 16 cubic feet of each ingredient.)

Shopping list

- **Peat Moss:**   16/8 = two full bales
- **Vermiculite:**   16/4 = four big bags
- **Compost:**   Whatever it takes to get 16 cubic feet of five different kinds. Forget weight, measure by volume.

More Shopping Lists for Different Sized Batches

If you had three 4×4 boxes (24 cubic feet total), you would need:

- two 4-cubic-foot bags of coarse vermiculite to equal 8 cubic feet.

- one 3.9-cubic-foot bale of peat moss (expands to 8 cubic feet).

- and 8 cubic feet from at least five different composts bags. If the bags are sold by weight only, estimate volume by comparing to similar sized bags that note volume.

If you had one 4×4 box and one 2×4 or one 3×3 box (12 cubic feet), and you wanted to mix up half of a batch to start with, you would add together just one 4-cubic-foot bag of vermiculite, half of a 3.9-cubic-foot bale of peat moss (or if you can find the 2.2-cubic-foot bales that expand to equal about 4 cubic feet loose), and two of the 2-cubic-foot bags of compost. If the compost comes in other sized bags, you may have to do a little arithmetic. That's enough Mel's Mix to fill one 4×4 box that needs 8 cubic feet plus one 2×4 box that needs four cubic feet, or one 3×3 box that needs 4½ cubic feet.

"**Y**our book, website and method are just fantastic."
—*Annie from New Jersey*

How to Mix

This is where making your Mel's Mix and filling your boxes starts to get fun. Mix it all at once if possible (storing any excess in recycled bags). But if it's too big a batch to handle, split it into smaller batches.

Here's a suggestion: Use a pair of scissors to cut open your bags carefully along the top so you can reuse them. At the same time explain to the kids the environmental three R's—reduce, reuse, and recycle. Our Square Foot Gardening system is a great example of:

1. reduce, by 80 percent,
2. reuse, save the bags, and
3. recycle plants in your compost.

Get a large tarp, at least 16×16-feet, and open it near your garden where you have all your boxes built and located. Make sure you have them in their final resting place—check with the boss one more time and ask, "Are you sure this is where you want all the boxes, dear?"

All of the three ingredients are dusty when dry, so do this when there is no wind. Don't do it in the garage, or you'll get dust all over your nice new car or workshop. Wear a painter's mask and have a hose ready with a very fine spray. Don't forget to have a few mixing tools ready like a snow shovel, a hoe, or a steel rake.

Empty the 5 bags of different kinds of compost in the center of a large tarp.

Count out the bags and boxes, do the math one more time and start opening the bags and pouring the contents out on the tarp without walking on the ingredients. Roughly mix the three ingredients as best you can as you pour it.

Then drag two corners of the tarp to the opposite two corners. You'll see the material roll over, mixing itself. When you've pulled

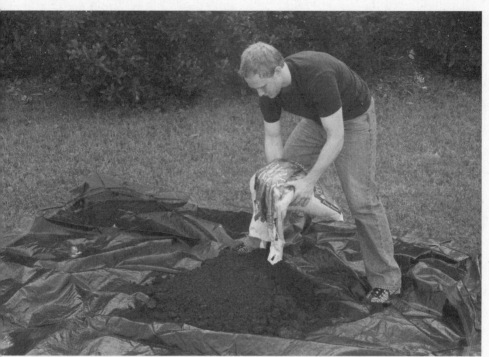

You should have a fairly large pile of blended compost.

To mix, take two corners of the tarp and drag the tarp over itself until the pile rolls to the edge of the tarp.

It helps to have two people do this.

Once the compost is well mixed, add your vermiculite.

Next, add the peat moss.

These ingredients can be dusty, so water them lightly before mixing. You may also want to wear a protective mask.

the tarp so that the mixture is almost to the edge, move 90 degrees and pull those two corners over. You just work your way around the tarp and repeat pulling corners together until your Mel's Mix is uniformly mixed. It's finished when you don't see any single material or one color.

Use the hose with a fine mist or spray to wet down any dust, but don't spray so much you make puddles or wet the ingredients so the mixture becomes too heavy to move easily. Don't let the kids play in the mixture, or they will crush the large particles of vermiculite. (By the way, I'd save a small plastic bag of vermiculite for seed starting. We'll get to seed starting in the next chapter.)

The next step is to fill the boxes, wetting down the mixed-in layers only as you fill it. Once the box is full and the top leveled off, don't pack it down. It will settle just right by itself.

If you have any leftover Mel's Mix, put it back in the empty bags you set aside for reuse. That extra Mel's Mix will come in handy to fill four-packs and use for transplants as well as extra to top off the boxes when the soil level settles. Turn the bags inside out if you want a plain look, label with a marker, and put them aside. Since you don't really water the mix until it's in the box, your stored mix will be fairly dry and lightweight to carry.

To fill other boxes, work with someone else to drag the tarp close to the new boxes. Don't try to carry shovelfuls of mix to the box as it will spill and be wasted. This is precious stuff. (Remember what Grandma always said, "Waste not, want not.")

That's also why we don't water the Mel's Mix in the tarp, but as you are adding it to the box—that way the remaining material in the tarp doesn't get so heavy that it is hard to drag. As soon as you add your grid to each box, you are ready to plant.

You have now completed the most important and rewarding step

MEL SAYS...

Don't wet the soil any more than is absolutely necessary; use a fine spray to reduce any dust. Soil becomes very heavy when wet, and it would be difficult to drag the tarp around your yard.

The finished Mel's Mix should look similar to this photo.

in SFG. If you followed the formula correctly, and didn't add any of your existing soil, it will stay loose and friable as long as you live and you will be so excited and happy. You may have to keep one square just for show; visitors to your garden will watch as you say, "Just look at this soil as you run your hands through it." Many of you will then add, "Here, you try it. Just feel this soil." (But don't become a pest.)

An Afterthought

I want to make doubly sure you got the message of this chapter, so I'd like to summarize the critical facts about compost. You need blended compost made from at least five different ingredients. Mix several different types of compost together if you buy your compost. Most commercial composts have only one or two ingredients because they are merely leftover waste materials or byproducts from an industrial or commercial operation. By themselves, they do not make a good ingredient in Mel's Mix.

However, the good news is, if you can find at least five of these individual composted materials you can mix them together to make a well-rounded blended compost ingredient for your Mel's Mix.

And if you did your job and got a blended compost made from at least five major ingredients, you will be blessed with the most wonderful garden you could ever imagine. **And no more work ever.**

How to Plant Your All New Square Foot Garden

Now we're getting to the interesting and fun part of Square Foot Gardening.

You've learned all of the basics. You've picked the size, shape, and location of your garden. You've built the frames, put in the Mel's Mix, and added the grids. Now it's time to plant. This chapter is going to instruct you on your plant choices, how to put your seeds in the garden with the proper spacing (it's as easy as Zip-Zap, Bing-Bing-Bing—you'll see), and growing your own transplants for the quickest, most dependable growth.

With your grid in place, it's easy to have a stunning garden by planting a different crop in every square.

Visualize the Harvest

In SFG, begin by visualizing what you want to harvest. This simple step
prevents you from planting too much. Picture a large plant like a head
of cabbage. That single cabbage will take up a whole square foot so you
can only plant one per square foot. It's the same with broccoli and
cauliflower. Let's go to the opposite end of the spectrum and think of
the small plants like radishes. Sixteen can fit into a single square foot.
It's the same for onions and carrots—sixteen per square foot. (Yet that's
a 3-inch spacing between plants, which is exactly the same spacing the
seed packet recommends as it says "thin to 3 inches apart.")

Small, Medium, Large, Extra Large

Think of these plants as if they were shirt sizes. Shirts come in all four
sizes: small, medium, large, and extra large, and so do our plants. It's
that simple.

The extra large, of course, are those that take up the entire square
foot—plants like cabbages, peppers, broccoli, cauliflower, and gerani-
ums. Next are the large plants—those that can be planted four to a
square foot, which equals 6 inches apart. Large plants include leaf lettuce, dwarf marigolds, Swiss chard, and parsley.

Several crops could be 1 per square foot if you let it grow to its
full size or it can be planted 4 per square feet if you harvest the outer
leaves throughout the season. This category includes parsley, basil,
and even the larger heads of leaf lettuce and Swiss chard. Using the SFG
method, you snip and constantly harvest the outer leaves of edible
greens, so they don't take up as much space as in a conventional garden.

Medium plants come next. They fit nine to every square foot, which
equals 4 inches apart. Medium plants include bush beans, beets, and
large turnips.

*For extra large plants,
locate seeds or plants
right in the middle of
your square.*

PLANT SPACING

Extra Large 1 Plant Placed 12 inches apart:	**Large** 4 Plants Placed 6 inches apart:	**Medium** 9 Plants Placed 4 inches apart:	**Small** 16 Plants Placed 3 inches apart:
Broccoli	Leaf Lettuce	Bush Bean	Carrot
Cabbage	Swiss Chard	Spinach	Radish
Pepper	Marigold	Beet	Onion

To help keep up with this, you may want to copy this chart so you always have it handy. Some people even have it laminated so they can take it outdoors without worrying about the weather destroying it.

Another way to get the proper spacing and number per square foot is to be a little more scientific and do a little arithmetic as shown below.

You can see that one, four, nine, or sixteen plants should be spaced an equivalent number of inches apart. This is the same distance the seed packet will say "thin to." Of course we don't have to "thin to" because we don't plant a whole packet of seeds anymore. So if you're planting seeds, or even putting in transplants that you purchased or grew from seed, just find the seed packet or planting directions to see what the

KID'S CORNER

ZIP, ZAP, BING, BING, BING

For nine per square foot, take two fingers, spread them apart, and draw two lines horizontally (zip, zap), which divides the square into thirds, and then two vertically, so that you've got nine sections. Folks from Texas like to use the "hook-em-horn"

sign using the trigger finger and little pinky finger.

For those with smaller hands (kids love doing this), use your thumb and the trigger finger, or take one finger and draw two lines separately going each way. Poke nine holes (bing, bing, bing) in the middle of your drawn squares and you're ready to plant your seeds.

It's even more fun marking the sixteen plantings per square foot. Remember, there is no measuring. Divide the square in half each way (eyeball it) by drawing lines in the soil with your finger, the same zip zap (one vertical line and one horizontal line, each divid-

ing the square in half) as described for four per square foot. Then, take two fingers, your trigger and middle fingers, and punch holes in the soil. They should be spaced about the same distance your eyes are spaced apart. Without poking yourself in the eye, hold your fingers up to your face so the fingers are spaced just about right, and then, mark your soil. In each of the four squares, go bing, bing, with your fingers, marking two holes each time so there are four holes in each small square.

For crops that can fit four to a square foot, divide the square into four sections and poke a hole in the middle of each section.

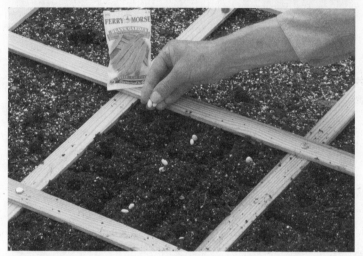

Plant seeds—just a pinch of two or three seeds depending on size—into the holes you poked into the squares.

distance is for thinning. This distance then determines whether you're going to plant one, four, nine, or sixteen plants.

Just because we're talking about measuring in inches doesn't mean you have to get out your ruler or yardstick, and you don't have to do any complicated measuring or figuring either. This is when the grid becomes handy. When your square foot is bordered by a grid, it's much easier to think one, four, nine, or sixteen plants in each square foot.

All you do is draw lines in the soil with your fingers! For one plant per square foot just poke a hole in the middle of the square with your finger. For four per square foot, draw a vertical and horizontal line dividing the square in half each way. The plants go right in the center of these four smaller squares.

How Much to Plant

I recommend, especially at the beginning, that you plant only what you want to eat. Occasionally try something new, of course, but especially at first only grow those vegetables and herbs that you normally eat.

Remember, plant each adjoining square foot with a different crop. Why? Here are several reasons:

1. It prevents you from overplanting any one particular item.

2. It allows you to stagger your harvest by planting one square foot this week and another of the same crop in two weeks or so.

3. It promotes conservation, companion planting, crop rotation, and allows better plant hygiene and reduced pest problems.

4. It automatically helps to improve your growing soil three times a year in very easy, small steps. Remember the saying, "Square by square, you'll soon be there."

5. Besides all of the above, it looks pretty.

Just like a patchwork quilt, the different colors, leaf textures, plant densities, shapes, and heights, plus the visible grid will give you a very distinctive, photo-opportunity garden. You'll just love and admire it everytime you see it.

Some people ask, "Why can't we plant all sixteen squares with leaf lettuce or spinach or Swiss chard or whatever we want to plant?" Oh, that's going right back to the single-row mentality. Square Foot Gardening begins with visualizing the harvest. It's very difficult to put in four tiny plants of Swiss chard and think that's going to be enough for the whole family, but one square of red and one square of green chard usually is more than most families eat. Proof of the pudding . . . how many bunches of Swiss chard did you buy last week or even last month? The stores have it, it's fresh, and it looks good, so why didn't you buy any more than you did? Well, it's the same answer as to why you shouldn't plant too much of one thing.

It's worth repeating here that the biggest problem for single-row gardeners has always been "I planted too much. I can't take care of it. It's too much work and I'm sorry now." All that has changed with SFG and you now have boundaries (the grid) and the opportunity to ask yourself, "For every single square foot I plant, is that enough? Do I really want more? Would it be better to plant another square foot of the same thing in a week or two or three?"

Time of Year

Keep in mind that you can build a Square Foot Garden anytime of the year—spring, summer, fall, and even winter. For most of the country, you could start planting in any season other than winter. What time of the year is it right now for you and where are you in the sequence of a yearly gardening cycle? Think of it like the movie theater before the main feature. You're all settled in with your popcorn, ready to devote your full attention to the movie. In the gardening year, this is usually the equivalent of springtime. What if you came in the middle of the picture? For gardening that would be summertime. You can still plant a warm-weather crop even if you missed the spring crop. If it's now fall, you can still start your SFG with a great cool-weather crop and get some valuable experience before next spring. Start **whenever** you get the urge to plant.

For convenience, we'll start with the beginning of the garden year for most of the country, springtime. (Some parts of the country, like Texas and Florida, can grow all year long. You lucky people.)

Seasonal Plants

You can get at least three crops a year in every square foot of your SFG. Every choice is going to be fun, exciting, and tasty. Of course, your selection depends on the time of year, and what you and your family need and want. There are two types of crops when you consider weather. The first are called cool-weather crops that do best in the spring and fall, but won't survive in the hot summer. The second group is the warm- or hot-weather crops that, you guessed it, don't do well in the cool weather of spring and fall, but thrive in the hot weather of summer.

Hardiness and Protection with SFG

SFG's size makes it very easy to protect your new plantings from an extra early or late frost. There's a lot more information about frosts and freezes in Chapter 9, especially if you are interested in extending the season, as well as ways to protect your plants so you can get more from your garden.

Plants aren't all the same, of course. They are just like people. Some can stand the heat, cold, or humidity better than others. We classify these as hardy, and those that can't handle it as non-hardy. Each of the four seasons has three time periods—the early season, midseason, and late season. If you're thinking about a spring crop, for example, there may be some vegetables that can only grow in the mid-part of the spring while others can tolerate a little more cold in the beginning of the season, but can't stand any heat at all near the late part of the season. Ittakes a little while to get used to which is which, and how best they fit in with your planting schedule.

Though the weather is never exactly the same every year, it helps to know a plant's hardiness. Don't worry—you'll learn it in time. This is not an exact science so relax if you're a beginner and just enjoy the ride. Don't expect to find a perfect list because how well plants thrive differs in different parts of the country and of course, different years, sometimes for no explainable reason. If you lose a few squares of something one year it's no big deal. It doesn't mean you're not going to be a great gardener.

Frost Dates

Although people like to celebrate the first day of spring (March 20th) according to the calendar, plants don't give a hoot about our calendar—they respond to weather. In the spring we need to know the date of the last frost in our area. That will help us determine when to plant. Each different crop—whether cool-season or warm-season—will need to be planted so many weeks before or after that last day of frost.

For plants, the fall growing season begins not with the first calendar day of fall (September 23rd), but with the first frost and continues until the first freeze of the fall. The average dates of your first and last frost depend on where you live in the country and the regional and local variations of weather. All we can do is go by the past and hope it will be similar this year. To help, the government collects dates for your area and calculates the average date from the past 100 years. Of course, the average is only a guide.

How do you find your local frost dates? The Internet is the best resource for detailed information. You can also call your local county extension agent or most area nurseries. To find your local extension agent, look in the Government blue pages for your county in your telephone book, then look for the heading "Extension of [your state] University."

Frost Date Websites

You can access your frost dates on any number of websites, by entering "frost dates" in the search engine. The best one I've found is **www.victoryseeds.com/hardzone**. This Internet site has the frost dates and hardiness zone maps for the entire United States as well as Canada, and links for hardiness zones for Australia, Europe, the Ukraine (in English), and China (also in English). The hardiness zone map for the United States is interactive, you just point to where you live and click, and you get the information. This site also links to your local university extension service. Let the experts advise you on the varieties that will do best in your local area.

Sequence of Growth

Did you know that plants grow and bloom everywhere in the same sequence? In other words, throughout the country, daffodils bloom in the springtime, then a little later tulips bloom, then it's time for the lilacs to bloom. (Did I leave out dandelions?) Start noticing the sequence in your location. It would include trees, shrubs, flowers, even weeds.

I read a book once about following spring north. It's theoretically possible that if you drive fast enough (and eat and sleep quickly), you could see nothing but tulips in bloom all the way from Georgia to Maine.

If you know what kinds of plants are summer crops (the most popular and well-known vegetables), it's easy to remember that everything else is a spring or fall crop. Summer crops include beans, peppers, eggplants, tomatoes, and squash. If you plant these when it's too early or cool, they'll either die or their growth will most likely be stunted for that year.

"You have got me so excited about gardening again; I love teaching SFG. It is so much more successful than other methods. I don't know why all gardeners and farmers aren't using it."

—Mike from Utah

Charts

I've designed charts for All New Square Foot Gardening so you'll know when to plant and in what order. These charts will guide you along, providing seed-to-sprouting times at certain soil temperatures. I've also included calendar charts that show, based upon area frost dates (assuming you have a frost), how soon before or after a frost you can plant a given crop. You'll find that some plants are very frost-hardy and can be planted much earlier than those that are just on the borderline. These are in the back of the book for easy reference.

Plan on a Fall Crop

As soon as the summer crop is finished, you're ready to plant cool-weather crops for the upcoming fall. These crops are frost-hardy, meaning that both young and mature plants withstand frost. The seeds you plant at the end of summer will sprout quickly since the soil is warmer. Transplants can begin outdoors and grow much faster than the same thing planted in the spring. Look at the charts; compare sprouting times for the same seeds in both spring and summer temperatures.

The fall crop gains an extra advantage from late summer weather. The problem with cool-weather plants in the spring is not cool weather but warm weather at harvest time. A plant's purpose in life is to reproduce seed, and the rising temperatures of an approaching summer make this happen sooner. As it does so, the plant's whole character changes. Many people don't realize that plants like lettuce put up a flower stalk, which then goes to seed. If you wait too long to harvest lettuce, the stalk will shoot up, and the same thing happens to other crops like cabbage. The head splits open, a stalk shoots up, develops flowers, and then turns to seed. It's nature's way of allowing the plant to reproduce, but the plant changes taste when this happens. All the energy goes toward the seed and the plant itself, as far as taste is concerned, becomes rather tough, coarse, and bitter.

In cooler weather, this process is delayed. The plant feels no urgency to complete the growing cycle. So in the fall, the plant slows its maturation process, allowing it to maintain flavor for a longer length of time as temperatures continue to grow cooler and cooler. If it's frost-hardy, it doesn't matter if it is the middle of fall and you start getting frost. Some plants can endure some freezing and still provide a crop for harvesting. Fall is a great time to plant if you put in the right crops.

Soil Temperature

Soil temperatures vastly influence sprouting times. For example, if you plant carrot seeds in the summertime when the temperature of the soil is between 60 and 80 degrees Fahrenheit, the seeds will sprout in less than a week. But if you plant the same seeds in early spring when the ground temperature is perhaps 40 degrees, they will take a month and a half to sprout. Just another 10 degrees warmer and they will sprout in a little over two weeks. The chart shows that when the soil is cold and freezing, no seeds will sprout. When it warms up to 40 only half of them will sprout; but as soon as it gets to 50 degrees, suddenly almost all of them will sprout and will continue right through the warmer temperatures of summer and fall.

What happens to seeds when they don't sprout because the ground is cold? They could rot, or fungus could attack them. They could break their dormancy and then go dry. They could be attacked by insects, or dug up by animals or birds. So, the quicker you can get them to sprout the better off they will be.

Spring, Summer, and Fall Crops

Some crops, like the cabbage family, take so long to grow that there isn't enough time to plant seeds directly in the garden and wait for the harvest. So you have to buy from nurseries or raise your own transplants indoors ahead of time.

The same situation applies to the warm-weather summer crops like tomatoes, peppers, and eggplants. They take so long to produce that you must plant your garden with transplants. The charts show this all in detail, indicating when to start seeds and when to transplant.

The fall crop is better for raising your own transplants because you will be able to start the seeds in the summertime, raise the transplants outdoors in your garden, and then move them into their permanent spot in the early fall for late fall harvest.

Starting Seeds and Growing Seedlings

There are plenty of advantages to growing your own transplants and storing the remaining seeds in their packet until next year. First, seeds cost pennies, while transplants cost dollars. There are many more varieties offered in seed catalogs than as transplants at the nurseries. The only setback is time because growing your own transplants depends on the time and work you can spare. If you're a brand new gardener, however, you may want to wait until next year to start your own transplants. Like everything else in life, we tend to go overboard and do too much and then it becomes a chore. Don't let it happen to you!

Storage of Seeds

If your seeds are stored properly, they will last for many years. Contrary to what the gardening industry would like you to believe, it is not necessary to buy fresh seeds every year or to pour out that whole packet of seeds all at once. SFG teaches you to plant just a pinch of seeds.

Although it's a great idea to start your own transplants from seed, this is an example of what not to do. It's not necessary to sow so much when you practice the SFG method.

Then store the rest. By planting just a pinch of seeds instead of a whole packet, you can save a lot of money by saving the excess seeds for next year's crop, and the next year's, and so on. Some seeds will last up to five years. Seed companies guarantee that a certain percentage will sprout; this number is always very high, usually up into the nineties. Of course the seed industry wants you to buy a fresh packet of seeds every year so they can stay in business. There's nothing wrong with that! But there's also nothing wrong with saving money with a more efficient system.

How to Store Seeds

What is the ideal storage condition for seeds? It is just the opposite of the moisture and warmth that make them sprout. You'll want to store them in a cool, dry place—the driest, coldest place in your home. Some people freeze their seeds. But I find they get moisture even if they are in a zip-lock bag because it never seems to be totally airtight. I prefer refrigerating them in a wide-mouth jar with a screw lid. Label your containers and store them in the refrigerator on a back shelf. In each jar place a desiccant packet from a film container, or medicine vial, or add a little powdered milk wrapped in a tissue to soak up any excess moisture in the jar.

Germination Rate

What happens to seeds that are in storage? As they grow older, their germination rate (the percentage that sprouts under ideal conditions) gradually diminishes. But the solution is very simple. Plant a pinch of seeds—just two to three—instead of only one to ensure that at least one will sprout. If your seeds are many years old, test the germination rate yourself or just plant three or five or however many seeds depending on how well they sprouted the year before. If you marked the sprouting rate on the packet, you can reasonably estimate how many to plant the next year.

What Did I Do Wrong?

Knowing that roots sprout first will help your seeds successfully grow. Here's why. Traditionally, gardeners hoed open a row, planted, covered, watered, and then walked away from their garden hoping for the best. If nothing grew, single-row gardeners thought the worst: "Maybe they were bad seeds. Or worse, maybe I'm a terrible gardener!" What all of these gardeners did not realize was that the seed might have already sprouted, perhaps after a week or two, and the root was heading down before the top could come up and break the surface. If the gardener gave up and quit watering, it is possible that their seed did die. Why? Because if the soil dries below the seed—in the root zone only 1 or 2 inches below the surface—the root will wither and die from lack of moisture. But if the gardener had kept the soil moist, then the seeds would have had a good chance to put the root down to support the plant and its new shoot.

Keeping Records

Many gardeners keep planting data—when, what, and where they plant, how long it takes to sprout, and how well their plants grow. It may sound like a lot of bookkeeping, yet some people enjoy recording their garden data and even set up computerized spreadsheets to make computations from this information. I don't bother to keep all these details myself, but if you enjoy it, this may help you learn faster and measure the progress more effectively.

Moving Plants

A SFG garden is small, and I've been able to change things around once they were all planted. It doesn't take much to move and re-plant something from one square to another if you think it would look better somewhere else. It's kind of like arranging a room of furniture and pictures on a wall. You can make all kinds of layouts and drawings even to scale, but I guarantee you once everything is in place, you'll change your mind.

Drop a Pinch

KID'S CORNER

WHICH SPROUTS FIRST
Which part of a seed sprouts first? Is it the top stem with its leaves? A fun children's book would have the tops popping out of the ground—looking around and if it likes what it sees and wants to stay, calling down to the root and saying, "Anchor me in." But that's a fairy tale.

For all seeds, the root sprouts first and goes down. How does it know to go down? Gravity! After the root gets started and secured with little feeder roots so it can start taking up moisture and nutrients, it calls up to the top and yells "all clear below" then the top sprouts and goes straight up against gravity.

We have learned about seed size and shape and storage and sprouting conditions. The next thing is to practice planting. You can do this indoors in the winter before you start your garden. Take different kinds of seeds from the tiniest to the largest and practice picking up and dropping a pinch of seeds onto a piece of white paper to count your results. This is really a lot of fun, almost a family game.

There is a very practical reason for doing this. When I tell people to just plant a pinch of seeds—two or three—I think I have given them all the instructions they need. But I always find so much variation in how many seeds they end up planting. It's in your finger dexterity, and you may need a little practice. If you are having trouble, you may even want to use a spoon for picking up that pinch of seeds. A white plastic spoon usually works great, especially if you're using darker colored seeds. If you scoop up too many, you can just shake a few back into the palm of your hand.

MEL SAYS...

SPECIAL CONDITIONS
Some seeds require special preparation or planting methods. These seeds are so few, though, that it's not worth going into detail. It's not something you have to remember or study because the seed companies, bless them, print any special instructions or requirements right on the back of the seed packet.

How Deep?

How deep should you plant a seed? This depends a lot on the size of the seed and the soil you plant it in. Generally speaking, a seed's depth is two to four times the thickness of the seed. It's important to place your seeds below a moist surface to prevent it from drying out. Too close to the surface and it can dry out from the hot sun. Once a seed receives moisture and begins sprouting (known as "breaking dormancy"), it will die if it dries out so don't forget to water regularly.

Too Deep Isn't a Problem

You don't have to worry too much about placing your seed too deep, in part because your Mel's Mix is loose and friable. If the seed is planted too deep for the kind of seed it is, as soon as it begins to receive moisture, nature will tell it, "Get going, buddy, put some roots down and start growing." That sprout can push right up through Mel's Mix because there are a lot of nooks and crannies and the soil is very easy to move. This is one of the hidden advantages of starting with perfect soil. It almost guarantees that all of your seeds will grow into plants.

Plant seeds 2 to 4 times the depth of their size. When they've sprouted, transplant them into four packs. When they're large enough and the right time comes, move them into their own square foot.

Time to Sprout

How long does it take to sprout seeds? The chart in the Appendix shows how many days it takes various types of seeds to sprout at various temperatures. In addition, what percentage can you expect to sprout? This chart can be valuable to you and should be used whenever you plant seeds. If you know ahead of time it's going to take 10 days for the seeds to sprout at the average outdoor temperatures, then you won't be a nervous Nelly every day wondering when, but you will know to keep that soil moist for those number of days. You can also judge from the percentage that will sprout at that temperature, how many extra beyond two or three seeds to plant to ensure one good healthy plant.

Presoaking

Before planting your seeds, give them a jump-start by presoaking them. While some can be soaked overnight, some fall apart after only an hour; it depends on the seed. Big seeds should be soaked for only about a half hour to an hour. Bean and pea seeds, which might look shriveled up, swell up and break in half if you soak them too long. Beware, water makes some seeds slippery. A plastic spoon can help you handle them.

Indoor Seed Sprouting

The easiest way to sprout seeds indoors is to place them on a moist paper towel. Then put the paper towel and seeds in a very shallow tray or dish; keep it moist (a plastic bag would be handy to maintain moisture) and in a warm place in the house. Check daily; when you see roots, it's time to plant. Rather than handling the seed at this point, carefully cut the paper towel into little squares, and lift each one out with a knife. Now you're ready to take it outside, plant it in your SFG filled with Mel's Mix, cover it, and give it a drink of water. You've just given your plant a head start—in about half the time. Instead of fourteen days, you may see a sprout coming up in just six.

Starting Transplants Indoors

Now it's time to decide whether you want to grow your own transplants indoors rather than direct seeding out-of-doors. To raise your own seedlings, you need a little bit of paraphernalia: Mel's Mix, a few cups and saucers, four-packs, and trays. Start your seeds in a little cup of vermiculite and transplant them into four-packs filled with Mel's Mix after they begin growing.

Seed Leaf

When you're sprouting seeds in a cup of vermiculite, I suggest you transplant them into the four-pack as soon as the tops have sprouted and you see the first two leaves called the seed leaves. Most garden experts say to wait until you have two "true" leaves, but I have found that if you wait until the set of true leaves develops, the roots have already grown so long and tangled that it's almost too late to transplant. The seed leaf comes first, and it's usually a fairly flat, large leaf that doesn't look like the plant's regular leaves. The first set of "true" leaves comes out next as the stem grows higher.

Lift By Its Ears

When the seeds have seed leaves and you're ready to transplant to the four-pack, carefully **lift** the plant by holding on to one of the seed leaves between two fingers. Then with your pencil, dig in the vermiculite, loosen it up, and lift the whole plant out—root and all—from the bottom while your other hand is holding the top of the plant by one of the seed leaves. Don't touch the plant stem, just the leaf. If the roots are very long, trim off the bottom third with a pair of scissors. Don't worry . . . you won't kill the plant. For every root you cut off, two new roots will sprout as it branches out, creating a much stronger plant.

To start seeds for growing your own seedlings, poke some holes into the bottom of a container. (This is a leftover plastic container shown in the photo.) Fill the container with vermiculite and pour water around the rim of the plate.

Add enough water until you notice a very slight color change to the vermiculite (it becomes darker). Pour a few seeds into the palm of your hand.

Pinch a few seeds with your thumb and forefinger.

Sprinkle the seeds across the surface of the vermiculite.

Cover the seeds with a thin layer of vermiculite (unless they need light to germinate; check the seed package).

After the seeds sprout, take your pencil and make a hole in one cell of your four-pack, or outdoors in your garden soil. Then lower the plant root down into the hole. Make sure the hole's big enough to hold the whole root. Take the point of the pencil and push the Mel's Mix around the plant. Plant it a little lower than when it sprouted. Give it some water, either from above for outdoors or from below for indoors in four-packs, and then give it shade immediately. Sun will kill that young seedling. In fact, if you're outdoors, always work in your own shadow, then make sure the plant has shade for at least a couple of days. (Refer to Chapter 4 for information about how to build shade cages.) Then you can let it have brighter light and then finally full sunlight.

Trim the Roots

When you place transplants into the garden, take a look at the roots to see if they are rootbound, in other words, if they've grown in a circle. My solution for a rootbound plant is to take that same pair of scissors and just cut off the bottom roots. Yes, the whole thing—the mass of roots and the soil. Then all the ends of the roots, wherever they are, will branch and send out little feeder roots. Lower the whole plant into the hole at the proper spacing in your outdoor garden.

You can trim excess roots by snipping them off with your garden shears.

Push the mix around seedlings to form a slight saucer shape in the mix. Because of the saucer shape, water is directed straight down to the roots.

Water Well

One caution: the plant and root should be very wet before you transplant into your SFG. Take your four-pack and let it float in a bucket of warm water until it sinks and there are no more bubbles coming up. That's when you know the plants are totally saturated with water. Then take it out, pop each plant out of its container, cut the root bottoms off, and plant it. Your garden soil should be moist, so you're not putting a wet plant into dry ground. Dry ground will suck the moisture right out of the roots.

Saucer-Shaped Depression

Next, push the soil back around the plant to form a slight saucer shape in the soil. Make sure you plant at the level of the soil, factoring in the slight depression of the saucer. Because of the saucer shape, water goes straight down to the roots. We don't want to water the rest of the square foot if we don't have to. How's that for conserving water?

Outdoor Seed Sprouting

The procedure for outdoor seed sprouting, transplanting into 4-packs, watering, and then planting into the garden is all the same, just in much nicer weather. Late afternoon on a cloudy day is the best time.

Hardening Off

Hardening off is the process of getting the plant adjusted to a new environment—like going from indoors to outdoors. It's important that your plants are acclimated gradually so they can get used to their new location and different weather conditions. This requires some effort because you don't want them out at night when it's cold or freezing and you also don't want them out in the burning hot sun in the daytime.

Regulate Sunlight and Heat

To help harden off plants, regulate the sun exposure. If it's hot out, place your plants out in the sunlight in the morning, but at noontime provide some shade. Let them receive direct sunlight in the early morning, shade at midday, and perhaps, when the sun starts down, a little more direct light in the afternoon. Now that's really pampering your garden plants. And don't forget the little drinks of water every now and then. Actually all that sun, then shade, then sun can easily be done with a shingle stuck in the ground at the right place and the right angle.

Can't Dry Out

To keep your newly planted seeds from cooking in the hot sun, cover the square with a piece of cardboard cut to fit in the grid. Estimate the soil temperature and sprout time (see the charts in the back), then write the sprout date and the date you planted it on the cardboard with a magic marker. Weight down the cardboard to keep it from flying away in the wind. Of course, you'll need to lift the cardboard before you sprinkle water on the soil surface to keep the soil moist, and then remove it a day or two before the sprout date.

Spacing

How many plants will fit into a square foot? The numbers are so simple and easy to remember: 1, 4, 9, or 16. If you like math, and who doesn't, you will recognize right away that these numbers happen to be the squares of 1, 2, 3, and 4. And, in addition to the fact that we're gardening in square foot plots, that's how Square Foot Gardening got its name . . . because it's as simple as one, two, three, four. The number of plants you grow in a square foot depends on a plant's size when it's fully grown. (Go to the chart in the back to see mature plant sizes.)

You can also figure it out very easily from the "thin to," directions on a seed packet. (Now, every time you read "thin to," you will think of me and say to yourself, "Why do the seed packets tell me to plant so many seeds only to go back and thin to just one plant?")

MEL SAYS...

PLANT SUPPORTS
If you are planting something that may need a plant support later as it gets fully grown, you might consider other plants that could share the same support and plant them in adjacent squares.

A Typical Garden

Let's plant one 4×4 and see how much we will grow in those 16 square feet. We'll start with tall plants on the north side of the box so they don't shade shorter plants. Then put some colorful flowers in each corner. Let's assume it is still springtime, but that we're past the last frost, so we could put four pansies in each corner using our favorite colors.

Carrots require little care until they're harvested. So let's plant two squares of different carrots in the center squares, one square of sixteen onions and a low-maintenance square of sixteen radishes in the center. Then we'll put one square of nine beets in an outside square because we'll harvest their leaves during the season and then finally pull the beet bottoms later. We can plant two or three varieties of leaf lettuce on the outside, depending on your tastes. In another square we could put sixteen chives, and four parsley plants in another, which would provide us a continual harvest. For more color we might want to put a square of red salvia along the back. And perhaps in one corner some dwarf dahlias, one per square foot. Or perhaps some nasturtiums spaced at one per square foot. One of the first things we would have planted in the spring is one or two squares of spinach, nine per square foot. Then depending on your family's taste we could have one or more squares from the cabbage family. That could be red or green cabbage, broccoli, or cauliflower. Keep in mind this is not the only 4×4 in the whole garden. So we don't have to put all the cabbage into one SFG. It's better to space them out throughout the garden—makes it harder for the cabbage moth to find them all.

Plans and Drawings

Remember I mentioned that some people feel a desire to think ahead and draw up a list of everything to be planted in their garden. Then there are even some people who want to assign those plants to spaces ahead of time. So it means drawing a chart, more or less to scale, of your garden and assigning those particular crops to each square foot. Despite being an engineer, who loves charts and diagrams, I don't usually do that. I just like to plant as I see fit. It's very easy to stand in the garden and as the square becomes vacant you just look around and decide it's time to plant another square of radishes. Or maybe you'd like to have some more beans, but this time you'll put in the yellow variety instead of green. It's also very easy to spot and plant where you'd like some color. I find it very easy to just bring home a four-pack of flowers I liked at the nursery and decide by looking at the garden where they would look best. But it's your Square Foot Garden, and you should do whatever makes you happy.

Replanting

Keep in mind that, as soon as you harvest, it won't be a big deal to replant because you're going to do it one square foot at a time. Once your newly planted garden starts maturing in the spring—for example, that square foot of radishes will be ready to harvest in four weeks— you'll be ready to replant just that one square. The season has changed and it's warmer, and most of your summer crops can now be planted. So your choices have increased and also most of the summer crop is fairly long-lived and will be in that spot through the whole summer season. As you replant you keep the same criteria in mind—taller plants on the north side to keep them from shading other plants, working your way to cascading flowers on the front corners to look pretty. Place plants that don't need much attention and only occasional harvesting like peppers on the inside, and shorter plants and those that need constant care or harvest to the outside just to make them easier to tend.

Weeding

This could be the shortest paragraph in the entire book. To start with, your Mel's Mix has no weed seeds in it, and any weeds that do sprout are easily observed because they're not in the proper space and they look different from the plants that are there. Because the soil is so soft and friable weeds come out easily—root and all. You have to weed about once a month. End of paragraph; end of story.

This is a good example of a rootbound container plant. You'll want to trim the matted roots before planting. (Don't worry, it's better for the plants anyway.)

Harvesting

Keep in mind that we harvest many of the crops continuously, if possible. For example, a leaf lettuce is not allowed to wait until it forms a large, mature head, but with a pair of scissors and a salad bowl you can continuously trim the leaves from such things as lettuce, chives, beets, Swiss chard, spinach, parsley, and even onion tops. As long as you don't take too much at one time, the plant will easily survive and thrive. Filling your salad bowl each day should not diminish the garden in any way. In fact, right after you harvest you'll find it hard to notice where you got everything and if anything is missing.

You've Learned the Basics

You've now learned all the basics of Square Foot Gardening. You've learned how it got its name—from the squares of one, two, three, four. You have also learned how many and what kind of plants fit into a square foot by memorizing, calculating, or by looking it up on the chart. You've learned how to zip zap in the soil to get the proper and exact spacing then start planting your seeds and transplants. Are we having any fun yet? Next chapter we're going to discuss how to maintain and harvest your SFG.

Okay, now it's time to go out to your garden and do something outrageous that will amaze or dumbfound any neighbor who might be watching you. Do you know how to do a rain dance?

Growing and Harvesting

MEL SAYS...

GROWING AND HARVESTING
- **Don't walk on your growing mix**
- **Only three tools needed**
- **Support your plants**
- **Weeds and other pests are not a problem**
- **Water the right way**

This is going to be a fairly short chapter because SFG requires so little maintenance once your garden is prepared and planted. You'll experience a continuous cycle of nurturing, harvesting, and replanting each year with no soil preparation and no weeding to do ever again. How does that sound?

All of the nurturing you'll need to do consists of providing necessary structural support for plants, ridding the garden of any tiny, occasional weeds or pests, and watering. You'll enjoy observing your garden's growth until harvest; every square is different because it was planted with a different crop at a different time. That's what makes SFG so interesting.

Care

When asked to name the greatest advantage of the All New Square Foot Gardening, most say it's tending their garden from aisles and never stepping on their soil. Like many others, I always wondered why we were taught to loosen soil with rototillers, shovels, forks, and hoes, only to walk all over it again packing it down.

So why are the experts still teaching us to do this? I say, just stop walking on your growing soil—it's that simple.

Keep It Loose

Let's think of some of the advantages of not packing your soil down. The plant roots need air and moisture, just like people. If you pack the soil down, it becomes more and more compressed (called compaction) and it becomes harder and harder for air to circulate through the soil making it more difficult for roots to grow. They may not die, but they certainly won't grow well. So why not provide them with nice, loose, friable soil like Mel's Mix? This way, water can percolate down and air can circulate.

These are the only tools you need for your All New Square Foot Garden. A trowel, a pencil, and scissors—that's it.

Three Tools

Another big advantage of SFG is that the number and cost of tools is reduced to almost nothing—you will only need three tools. Just think, you no longer need a rototiller! Eliminate that cost and you now have an extra $1,000 in your pocket. And you don't have to hire someone at $50 every year to plow for you. You don't even need a shovel or rake or any of those special digging tools that have been invented to dig up the tough soil. Gardening "experts" will tell you to go out and buy the best tools you can find because they will last longer, but they also cost more. With SFG, you no longer need any of those big, expensive, heavy-duty tools that take so much energy to maneuver—they're suddenly obsolete.

A Trowel, A Pencil, and Scissors

The first tool of the three tools you need is a trowel. I've found that the one-dollar variety is really the best buy. They're attractive, strong, and neat looking. They have all the features of a six dollar trowel. So instead of just one, now you can afford six—one for every SFG box! Why not buy an assortment of colors? You can have one in every box just sitting there waiting so that you don't have to go looking for a tool when you walk by and see a square that is ready for replanting. Of course, if you see an occasional weed, your big, strong weeding tools are your own thumb and forefinger!

The trowel is for transplanting, for mixing in an added trowel full of compost when you replant each square foot, and for loosening up and turning over the Mel's Mix in an individual square foot or even an entire 4x4. In the spring you won't believe how perfect the soil will be **if** you follow the Mel's Mix formula and start with a perfect soil.

> ## PENNY PINCHER
>
> I like to buy children's pointed scissors in August when you can find back-to-school sales. Usually I can purchase them for about fifty cents—an affordable price that allows for several pair around the garden.

The other two tools you'll need are a pencil (yes, that's a tool) for poking holes and lifting out young seedlings for transplanting, and a pair of scissors for harvesting beet, lettuce, or Swiss chard leaves for supper, cutting off dead blossoms, and snipping off extra seedlings if more than one seed sprouts in a hole. Because SFG tools are so simple and inexpensive, I love to splurge and keep one of each at every 4x4. That way, I never have to look for a tool.

It would be fun to list all the tools that you no longer need if you have a SFG. In fact, you could probably just go into your garage or toolshed and see them all right there—poor, lonely tools. Maybe you have some old-fashioned single-row friends who just can't give up all that hard work and could use some extra heavy-duty tools. You could rent them out and maybe make a few bucks.

that hard work and could use some extra heavy-duty tools. You could rent them out and maybe make a few bucks.

Optional Acccessory

Although you only need three tools, you might want to invest in a kneeling pad. Unless your boxes are placed on tabletops, your most frequent position while gardening will be kneeling. For less than four dollars, you can buy a kneeling pad that is comfortable and durable. There's no need to buy the fancy ones that strap to your knees. They're terribly uncomfortable and will end up hanging in your tool shed along with the other lonely tools.

PENNY PINCHER

You can even make your own kneeling pad out of scrap carpeting. If you have some leftover indoor/outdoor carpeting, it won't matter if it gets wet; it dries quickly and folds up nicely to make a great kneeling pad. It wouldn't hurt to have a few of these pads scattered throughout your SFG. They are available as scrap or samples at any place carpeting is sold.

Weeds

SFG has few or no weeds. But how? Weeds plague every garden, right? First, there are no weed seeds in peat moss or vermiculite. Next, any seeds that were in the ingredients you added to the compost pile will get cooked and killed in that 150 degrees Fahrenheit temperature as the pile heats up. If you prepare the bed properly and line the bottom of the box with landscape fabric, no weeds will sprout from the bottom. Since we are not using our ground soil, which is filled with weeds, the only possible weed seeds in our SFG might have blown in, and as soon as they sprout, you will see them because they are out of place.

First, remove any weeds or grass from inside your box, then lay down landscape fabric as a weed barrier. This will be your "best friend" against future weeds.

Your two fingers will do the rest, pulling out the weed, roots and all. Compare that to what you've experienced with your existing soil. Anytime the existing soil anywhere in the country is left alone, it sprouts weeds. Which system would you like to have in your backyard?

I See You

How can you tell if a new sprout is a weed? First, it's not in the proper space among your little transplants. Remember one, four, nine, and sixteen.

If it is out of place (and I'll bet you were careful to make sure your spaces were correct in that square foot), you'll pull it out of that soft Mel's Mix without a problem.

Pests and Plant Problems

The only way to intelligently answer the questions we get about pests and plant problems requires knowing the weather, growing conditions, history, and present gardening condition in an area. If the question came from my county, I'd give a great answer. But when it comes from across the country or anywhere in the world, it's difficult to give an accurate answer.

County Extension Agents

There is a good solution. Some of our tax dollars go to train and maintain a staff of horticultural experts in every county in the country —the county extension service agents. In addition, the county extension agents train another group of neighborhood volunteers called "Master Gardeners," who then go out in the community helping others by answering their questions. It is a great service, and we often refer questions to the agents and their staff. If your question is about pests or problems or even the best varieties to grow in your area, you couldn't find a more informative source. To find your local extension agent, look in your phone book in the Government blue pages, find your county, and then look for the heading "Extension of (your state) University," don't look under "Agriculture."

The only problem I have with the county agents is that most of them are trained in our agricultural colleges, which still teach single-row farming and hand-me-down gardening. So, they are not the best source for answers to SFG questions. You'll have to come to us for those questions.

To summarize pests and problems, try not to worry about them. Enjoy your garden. If one square gets devastated, pull it up and re-plant it with something else. If you didn't use the protective structures of Chapter 4, try them out next season to help eliminate your problems.

"I've lived my life doing the backbreaking work of single row gardening—this is so much better!"
—*Gina from Kentucky*

Which Plant Varieties?

Quite often people will ask questions like, "Which are the best varieties of potatoes or carrots to grow in my corner of the state?" These questions can only be answered by your local expert—the county extension agent. They are always up-to-date on all the new varieties and what grows best in their area. Keep in mind if you have a question about any of the vine crops, you will want to train them to a trellis, while most single-row gardens allow them to sprawl.

Notice how easily vine crops such as pole beans climb the trellis netting all by themselves. Other vine crops, such as tomatoes, need a little help from you each week.

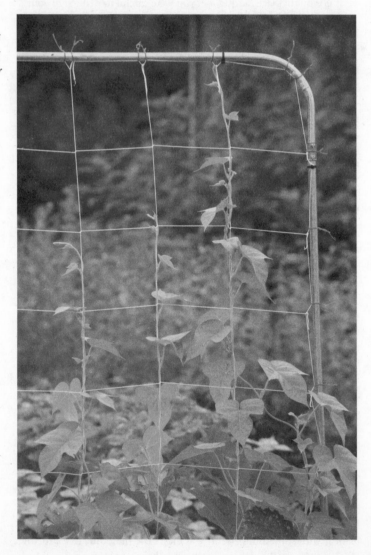

Support Your Local Plants

Some plants, such as root crops and low-growing salad crops, need no support, so there is nothing to do for them. The taller crops might need a little help, however, depending on whether they are a leaf or head crop like Swiss chard or cabbage. If a heavy wind and rain or hailstorm knocks them over, simply straighten them up and push a little extra soil around the stem.

Too Top Heavy

The plants that usually need a little support are the summer crops like peppers, okra, eggplant, corn, and bush tomatoes. Those can easily be supported by using a U-shaped wire support cage or horizontal fencing or netting suspended across the entire 4×4 garden, held tight by four corner posts. (See Chapter 4 for construction details.) The same support technique will also work for tall flowers like gladiolus, giant marigolds, and tall dahlias. One of the reasons we provide plant support is the soil mix is so loose and friable that the tall plants need a little help.

Watering

Plants need water just like people do. Everyone asks, "How do you water and how much?" My ideal way to water is ladling out a cup of sun-warmed water from a bucket that can be left in the sun next to your garden. Gently lift the bottom leaves of the plant and, with your other hand, ladle a cup of that water into the depression around the plant. With a saucer-shaped depression in the soil, the water will soak right down to the roots instead of rolling away from the plant into other parts of the garden.

We do get a few people who say, "Oh that would take too long." But they've failed to think about the fact that, first, their garden is only a fraction of the size that it used to be. That means 80 percent of the watering you used to do is no longer needed and was actually wasted. Next, you're not watering the tops of the plants or the leaves, so you're not promoting fungal diseases and other problems. You're keeping the water where it will do the most good—around the base of the plant where it can travel down to the root system.

The soil consistency of your Mel's Mix is already 100 percent of materials that hold moisture. When you water, it goes right into the soil around the root system and stays there. The root system is going to be able to drink up the water when and in the amount needed. Is this a major advance in water conservation or what? Hello, conservationist, are you listening?

When your plants need a drink, just dip a cup of water from your 5-gallon bucket of sun-warmed water, and pour it in the saucer-shaped depression.

And why sun-warmed water? One answer is that it's for the same reason people don't like to take a cold shower. The more scientific reason is plants can absorb nutrients in the soil much faster and grow better if the soil and water temperature are warmer. In spring and late fall, sun-warmed water helps warm the soil. Remember the chart in the Appendix showing sprouting times in various temperatures. The warmer the weather, the faster they'll grow and the quicker you'll harvest. That's why people have greenhouses. If you build a structure to form a miniature greenhouse around your SFG, the radiant heat from the sun will warm the soil from the surface down. But simply pouring warm (not hot) water into the soil means the warmth tends to go a little deeper—and even quicker—than the sun baking the surface of the soil.

Don't Drown Me

Invariably gardeners water plants too much, perhaps out of kindness or fear that they will fail. So they think, "Oh, I'll give it a little extra. It won't hurt." Usually it did hurt with local soil that didn't drain well, but it won't if you have a Square Foot Garden where the soil drains excess water. Most people don't realize that plant roots need air as well as moisture. Lucky for you, Mel's Mix allows air into it because it's loose and friable. (Chapter 5 tells you how to make Mel's Mix.)

With Mel's Mix you cannot overwater. Remember the sponge? Each little piece can hold moisture so a plant root can grow around that piece and take out the moisture when needed. When that little sponge gets saturated, the rest of the water drains right out through the bottom. That's how Mel's Mix works, and that's why you never have to worry about giving your plants too much water.

But because your soil mix drains readily when saturated, it also has a tendency to dry out quicker than most garden soils. Regular soils

soils stay saturated, so single-row gardeners may be used to turning on the sprinkler or flooding the garden twice a week and that's it. Your All New Square Foot Garden is different. You have to water a little more often and pay more attention to watering.

The secret, of course, is looking at the plants. After a while you'll be able to walk past your 4×4 garden box and immediately spot any square foot that needs water. Perhaps the plants will be slightly wilted. Maybe they'll be just a little droopy or their color will be a little off. You merely water those square feet right then and there because your bucket of warm water is always right next to your garden. And because you're dipping a cup in the bucket you're not going to get yourself all wet and dirty.

Think of your plants in your garden the same as you do your children. If they've been out in the hot sun and playing hard and one of them looks a little droopy and wilted, you know right away to inspect the child a little closer to make sure he or she is properly hydrated.

MEL SAYS...

With Mel's Mix you cannot overwater. I repeat: you cannot overwater.

Nurture Your Plants

I suggest watering by hand because it allows you the time to nurture your plants. You're able to stop and notice how your plants are growing. You can appreciate their beauty and color, notice their blossoms and fruit. It tells you when the plant is going to be ready for harvest. It's a satisfying feeling to work in your garden with each plant. You're not standing off in the distance with a hose, which is very impersonal. You're not opening a big valve and letting the sprinkler system take over or the irrigation water come in. (And guess what? Irrigation water is filled with weed seeds. Have you folks who live in states that irrigate ever wondered why you have to weed your single-row garden so often?) Even a drip irrigation system is impersonal—though, I must admit, efficient.

Too Much

Existing watering systems give all different types and sizes of plants the same amount of water at the same time. This is not only very impersonal; it's also very inefficient. If our farmers did that we'd have water shortages all around the country. Hey, wait a minute, we do have water shortages all around the country!

How Much

In conclusion, only water as much as each plant needs. And the best way to tell is from experience—the same way you know your child needs a drink. Yes, it does take a little bit of experience to raise a family, but gaining this experience brings a lot of pleasure.

Alternate Watering Methods

A Hose

For those who want to use a more traditional method, there is always the hose. Yes, it's a nuisance to get out or put away, and in row gardening it always seemed to be knocking plants down as it has to be dragged around the garden. Another advantage to SFG boxes is the hose won't do that anymore as the box corners keep the hose from crushing the plants.

If you do use a hose, make sure you have one of those shut-off valves right at the end of the hose so you have complete control of the force and amount of the water. There are many short and long extension hand wands that come with a spray nozzle. This also allows you to water directly under your plants, and the nozzle on the end of the wand can be poked down and worked around the lower leaves of the plant so that most of the plant remains dry.

Leave an extra length of hose coiled in the sun to help warm the water up a little, maybe just to take the chill off tap water, but you have to be careful at the start if it's hot out and a hose full of water has been laying in the sun for some time. You don't want the water to be too hot. Do what you do when giving the baby a bottle—test the water on your wrist.

Drip, Drip, Drip

A very efficient way to water your SFG is with a drip irrigation system. I know it was designed for row gardeners, but it can be adapted for SFG just as easily. The only problem I have is it sort of takes away the nurturing and close attention paid to your plants. If you just turn a valve or worse yet, a mechanical timer turns the water on and off, you never get close to your plants and they will miss you.

But I must admit the watering gets done very efficiently and effectively. Try running small soaker tubes spaced every 6 inches the length of your box for complete coverage of every square foot.

Lawn Sprinkler Systems

Some people tell me they have located their SFG on the lawn, and they have an underground sprinkler system that goes on and off automatically. What should they do, they ask? What can you do—rip up the lawn or turn off the system? No, you just live with it. I tell them to make do with what they have and just keep a bucket or two around for special plants as needed.

Harvest

Harvesting your crop is the culmination of the gardening experience. The harvest should be a joyful and exciting time because, after all, this is why you're growing all these plants in the first place.

Too Much

The problem with traditional gardening is that there is too much to harvest all at once. If you plant an entire row of something all at once, it's all going to be ready to harvest all at once, and it becomes an overwhelming task. Not so great for the home gardener who just wants dinner tonight, not a month's worth of lettuce in one day. So, after the first few pickings, the rest becomes all drudgery.

Control That Planting

Everything is different with a SFG. Now, every time you begin to plant something in your SFG, look the item up in your SFG book to find how many to plant per square foot. Prepare the soil, smooth it out, do the zip, zap, bing, bing, bing, bing to mark the spacing. Now, select the varieties you want from your seeds, pour some into the palm of one hand, and plant a pinch in each hole. As you smooth the soil over the seeds, water with a fine spray. Then ask yourself, "Do I want any more than sixteen radishes all at once? They'll be ready in four weeks and they'll all come to harvest within one week." Usually the answer is "No. I really don't want any more than this. I'll wait a week or two to plant another square foot of radishes somewhere else." Right then and there you can see one of the huge advantages of your grid establishing boundaries and SFG giving you automatic control—simple and easy.

Remember that the SFG theory is to visualize the harvest. Ask yourself, "How much do I need for one or two weeks?" Then only plant that much. It takes about a minute.

A Little of This, A Little of That

You don't have to wait for the plant to mature to its maximum size. Go out at harvest time (which might be a half an hour before lunch or dinner) with your pair of scissors and a small basket or salad bowl, and cut off a few outer leaves, perhaps one from each plant. To harvest a varied salad, just take four lettuce leaves, parsley leaves from another, and perhaps beet greens from another. Each square may contain a different variety and color of lettuce. You might pull one radish and one carrot, even though they've only grown to half size, wash them off in your bucket of sun-warmed water, put the tops in the compost bin, and then continue around your Square Foot Garden taking just a little bit here and a little bit there of this and that. Soon your harvest basket is full and you look at your garden and cannot even see that anything is missing.

"I had always been a little afraid of composting, but Mel makes everything so logical and easy to understand."
—Karen from Utah

Snip, Snip

Continually harvest any type of leafy vegetable—like leaf lettuce or Swiss chard—by snipping a little here and a little there throughout the season. This can't go on forever because the plant, especially cool weather plants, will eventually go to seed. When it sends up a seed stalk, the plant has completed its growing season and its use for harvesting. Take one last harvest, remove what's left over, and prepare that square foot for replanting—unless you want the kids to see how a lettuce or radish plant produces seed.

Harvest and Replant

With Square Foot Gardening, you're only dealing with one square foot at a time. To paraphrase the words of Dr. Robert Schuller, "Inch by inch, anything's a cinch." With SFG, our saying is going to be "square by square, you'll soon be there." As soon as you finish harvesting one square foot, it's time to prepare the soil and plant a new crop. Just take out any debris like dead leaves, stems, or roots—you can place these in your compost bin—then add a trowel full of compost (hopefully it's homemade) to the square, turn the soil over with the trowel, smooth it over, and you're ready to replant. You can do all of that in 60 seconds!

Replanting

Now it's getting more interesting and fun because you will be able to choose what you want to replant in every single square foot all through the garden season. Remember, you can get at least three crops a year in every square foot. So, multiply your number of square feet by three and there are a lot of choices to make! Every choice is going to be fun, exciting, and interesting. Of course, what you select depends a lot on what time of the year it is and what you can use and enjoy.

A Little Now

Whether you're planting, harvesting, maintaining, or watering you don't need hours and hours to enjoy your garden. Because you can do a little bit here and a little bit there, you can do it anytime of the day—even on your way out the door! If you see a few tiny weeds growing, pluck them out; give a drink of water to any plants that appear a little droopy or wilted (remember your bucket of sun-warmed water is right there and so is your trowel if you need to loosen the soil). It's like straightening a crooked picture as you walk down the hall, jotting a note to someone who will be coming home soon, or putting something away in the re-frigerator. These are things you can do right then and there. And they're fun things to do. No heavy work. No getting all dirty and sweaty.

A Wonder

If your garden is close to the back door or kitchen door, you'll proba-bly use it much more. You'll enjoy the fresh greens and salad more often, eat healthier, and feel better. SFG could be part of a weight-loss program, if you ask me! On top of all that, you'll have fun doing it! Don't forget to share the fun with your spouse, children, or grand-children—the wonder of growth and harvest is priceless. Harvest a few small plants with a child, and that child will remember the experi-ence forever.

Next Crop

When the summer is finished, you're ready to plant a fall crop, which will be a cool-weather crop. Go through the whole quick process of picking out any debris, adding a trowel full of compost, mixing it in, smoothing it over, and deciding what's next. There goes another minute out of your busy life. How about spinach? Check the spacing, get the seeds out, soak them for a little while, pop them in the ground, smooth them over, water, and you're all finished. Another minute gone, but you are creating life. You've now planted three crops in one square foot in only one year. You started with a root crop, replaced it with a fruit crop, and finally, in the fall, added a leaf crop. In addition, you practiced soil improvement three times in one year—square by square.

Rotation Not Critical

The nice thing about SFG is you are also practicing crop rotation without even knowing it. Crop rotation is very important in traditional row gardening when dealing with existing soils that have very few nutrients in them—nutrients that can quickly be depleted by planting and replanting the same crop year after year in the same soil. When you begin gardening with a healthy, rich soil like Mel's Mix, crop rotation is really not critical. Mel's Mix gives you a garden soil that is 33 percent compost, which has all the nutrients and trace elements that plants need. But crop rotation is still a good idea for insect and pest control in addition to soil nutrients. If you grow the same thing continuously in the same place, eventually pests or diseases may take over since they have lived and played in that spot for so long. But if you replant every square three times a year, SFG is going to be no picnic for them. They will have to move every two months. I'll bet they will go somewhere else to set up residency. How about your row gardener next door that laughed at you when you started building your boxes?

Add Color

One more thing. Now that you've become an accomplished gardener one square at a time, you've improved the look and landscape of your garden and perhaps even your yard and patio. When you decide you need a little color over here or there, you may put in a summer crop of flowers—perhaps pink petunias—you become a designer. Just think—you're enjoying a painting in progress when you garden the All New Square Foot Gardening way!

What are some of your favorite flowers or herbs? Plant them among your veggies for added color and interest.

Vertical Gardening

‌|ı|ıı|ı|ıı|ıı|ı|ıı|ı|ıı|ıı|ı|ıı|ı|ıı|ıı|ı|ıı|ı|ıı|ıı|ı|ıı|ı|ıı|ıı|ı|ıı|ı|ıı|ıı|ı|ıı|ı|

By now, you might feel that the 80 percent reduction in size, the no fertilizer needed, the growing in only 6 inches of Mel's Mix, or even the no digging of your existing soil ever again are all that you could ask from your All New Square Foot Garden.

In addition, you might say that most people would think that all of the above is amazing and earth-shattering (well, okay, how about just impressive), but this topic, "Vertical Gardening," is downright spectacular.

How It Happened

Here's a quick flashback to 1976 when this retired engineer took up gardening. I developed SFG but as I looked at tomato plants growing in pots on decks and in single-row gardens, I knew my work wasn't complete. Tomatoes are not only America's favorite vegetable to grow, but they also take up the most room and cause quite an unsightly mess by the end of the season if they are allowed to sprawl all over the ground. There are also the complaints of slugs getting in and ruining all of the tomatoes as well as gardeners stepping all over the vines and crushing them when trying to harvest the fruit. The whole idea of growing tomatoes this way seems very non-productive. At the time, the only cages available were too short and too weak to solve the problem.

I said, "This is no way to treat a tomato. We can't let it lie down and sprawl all over the ground. It should be allowed to stand up straight and tall so that it can be proud of itself and a benefit and credit to the community."

Six months later my vertical frame was designed, tested, and put into operation. It was an All-American model made from rigid German steel conduit and Japanese twine. It was so strong that it held up through rain, sleet, snow, and heavy September storms when the tomato plant filled the entire frame and was loaded with red, ripe tomatoes.

MEL SAYS...

Why Should You Grow Vertically?
- It's spectacular.
- It saves space.
- You grow better crops.
- It adds a third dimension to your SFG.
- It costs less then you could imagine!
- It lasts for years.

How Do You Grow Vertically?
- Build a super strong steel frame.
- Attach nylon netting.

Where Do You Grow Vertically?
- Along the north edge of your 4×4.
- Next to any fence or building wall.

When Do You Grow Vertically?
- Anytime before vine crops start sprawling.

"I couldn't believe the amount of vegetables it raised."

—Dan from Texas

After growing tomatoes this unique and attractive way for several years, I began thinking about the other vine crops that spread all over the garden. Could they be grown the same way? First I tried pole beans (a no-brainer), then cucumbers and peas. Then even winter and summer squash. They all worked and grew well, and they looked just great growing on a vertical frame. And I was so pleased with the results of growing vine crops this new way that I said, "This is a good thing," and included the method in my first book on SFG.

But since then—**Wow!** You should see the vertical gardens now. The pumpkins, all kinds of melons (including the new smaller watermelons), and all of the really big squashes grow 7 feet in the air.

Vertical Gardening

A few years ago at our display gardens in Utah, we were growing 35-pound pumpkins 7 feet in the air. We made the vertical frames 8 feet above the ground for no other reason than we wanted to show off and demonstrate how tall they can be! Now this was a spectacular sight, and many people have wanted to know how they could accomplish this same feat in their own backyard.

We usually refer to vertical gardening as "Advanced SFG." But, really, as soon as you master the basics of Square Foot Gardening, you can enjoy growing crops vertically. And you will be the envy of the neighborhood when you do.

Growing vertically not only saves space but it also adds another dimension of beauty to your garden.

Picture This

Can you just picture a wall of green in your garden filled with vine crops like tomatoes, cucumbers, pole beans, even melons and squash? All the colorful fruit just hanging there waiting to be picked! No sprawling plants all over the ground with their fruit lying on the soil getting all dirty and eaten by slugs. These walls of green can even be located so they hide any unsightly areas of the yard or garage. They can even give you some privacy to keep neighbors from peering over the fence to look at your SFG. It's not only a spectacular sight, but those plants will be up in the air getting better sunshine and air movement. They'll produce a more useable harvest for you with nothing wasted. To top all that off, each plant will only take 1 or 2 square feet of garden space and grow perfectly well in your 6 inches of Mel's Mix. Another big advantage is you can do all this standing up— no bending, kneeling, or squatting down to tend your plants.

To construct a vertical frame, you need: two 5-foot electrical conduit pipes ($^1/_2$-inch diameter); one 4-foot conduit pipe ($^1/_2$-inch diameter); two 18-inch long rebar supports of $^1/_2$-inch diameter; screwdriver; hammer; two elbow connectors; and trellis netting.

Extending the Seasons

We gardeners like to bend reality a bit. Nature says, "You can't plant now, it's too cold." But we say, "Wanna make a bet?" This chapter will show you on how to get the most out of your garden each year by pushing the envelope on nature's conditions. With a variety of easy-to-make implements, your garden can grow 30 to 50 percent more produce each year. And in addition to the extra food, it extends the beauty of the garden and the satisfaction of the gardener. However, this idea isn't necessarily for the first-time gardener unless you've got a lot of time, a natural talent, and a lot of confidence.

Nature gives us our gardening cues as the seasons change. We're going to use those seasonal cycles as our framework for this chapter.

But first, why would you want to extend your seasons? Well, would you like to pick the first tomatoes on the block? Would you like a garden-fresh salad on Thanksgiving? Your answer to these questions will help you determine how much work you want to put into extending the growing season because growing out of season does require more time and effort.

> "**F**antastic! It very much appeals to my innate sense of organization and efficiency."
> —Jeff from North Carolina

Lengthen Season by 50 Percent

In most parts of the continental United States, the average growing season runs from May to September. This means that most gardeners grow vegetables during an average of six months out of a possible twelve. When these six months are extended by an additional two months, the growing season is extended by 33 percent. A three-month extension provides a 50 percent increase—a worthwhile goal that can be achieved easily and inexpensively. Gardeners gain a great sense of accomplishment from these increased yields, and modern homesteaders and food preservers find it an absolute blessing.

Square Foot Gardeners don't have the negative experiences associated with doing all that hard work when they garden, so they look forward to more gardening and want to lengthen the growing season.

For them, gardening isn't a test of endurance. It's a pleasant experience. They don't want to know how soon they can quit, but how long they can continue experiencing the joy of gardening!

Don't think you **must** extend the season to be an accomplished gardener. Sometimes it's just as good to sit back, relax, and just "go dormant" for a while. Instead of gardening you could be satisfied and save time and work.

It's your decision. But if you think it's time to trick nature into feeding you year-round, then read on! The rest of the chapter will explain what to do each season to extend your harvest from cool-weather and warm-weather plants.

Extend the Harvest by Growing Out of Season

The obvious way to extend the garden year is to start earlier than usual and keep the plants growing later. Cool-weather crops can be grown in two extra plantings for a longer season. The first planting is made in the early spring and will mature in the cool weather of late spring. The second crop of cool-weather plants can be planted in late summer to mature in the late fall.

If you want to jump-start your garden, try starting your own seeds. But with the SFG, you won't need all this expensive equipment and you won't have so many plants to take care of.

Since early spring and late fall can bring some rather severe weather, growing out of season is simply keeping the cold temperatures away from your plants. To do this, it's important to provide these crops with the extra protection they need from the elements.

By covering and protecting your crops, you are basically creating an artificial environment. After all, that is what a greenhouse does—it keeps the cold air out but lets the sunlight in. What more could a plant want?

In addition, all of the summer or hot-weather crops can be started two to three weeks earlier than normal and they, too, can be extended up to a month beyond their normal season in the fall. Then, an extra planting of lettuce, spinach, and radishes can be grown during the hot summer months that are normally considered out of season for these two crops. Sound like a lot of work? With Square Foot Gardening, it's easier than you think. It all depends on you providing protection from the sudden and harsh temperatures and weather.

Box with Cage

Since a Square Foot Garden takes up so little space, it is relatively easy to protect your crops.

While special techniques that provide extra protection may vary with the season and the variety of vegetable, they are quickly learned and easily practiced. Chapter 4 explains how to build a special box and the various kinds of protective cages. These structures make it possible to moderate the climate in that box so you can stretch your growing season at both ends.

Early Spring

A great time to extend the growing season is early spring before anyone else is out gardening. Begin by warming up the soil in your SFG boxes. Spread clear or black plastic over the top of the soil, and weigh it down with a brick in each corner. After a couple of sunny days, take the cover off, lift the grid out, and mix up the soil with a trowel so the warmer surface soil is moved down below and the colder, deeper soils are raised to the top. Then replace the plastic covers. This is no big deal since your Mel's Mix is loose and friable at all times of the year. Besides, the soil is only 6 inches deep. How much work could that be?

Jump Start Your Seeds

If you want to get a quicker start and earlier growth, try sprouting your seeds indoors, and then transplanting them into individual containers when they are very young. Before the plants get too large, harden them off before planting them outdoors in your spring box.

Spring

For your first spring planting, set up a spring box with a storm window cover or the PVC type structure over any garden square where you'll be planting an early crop so the sun will start warming the soil. Do this about four weeks before it's time to plant your seeds. For a double-quick soil warm-up, cover the soil with clear or black plastic, and then remove it before planting. Or you can use plastic covered cages over individual squares around the garden instead of the entire 4×4-foot area. When the weather is warm enough, transplant the plants you've grown into the open garden squares. They can also be left to grow where they were planted by removing the protective cage from the squares.

MEL SAYS...

You must check your spring plant boxes every day in sunny weather. If your plants begin to wilt or if the soil dries to a depth of 1 inch, it's time to water. Water with a cup of sun-warmed water.

Climate Control

When you're using a spring box on your early crops, remember that fresh air has to get in and you have to vent out the hot air that builds up on sunny days even in cold or freezing weather.

Heat builds up quickly in the boxes on sunny days. As the weather warms up, slide or lift the cover open a little farther each week until you can remove it entirely. (Don't try to prop up a glass storm window with sticks; believe me, the wind will blow it down whenever you're not around.) A light frost won't hurt most cool-weather crops, but too much heat will cook them. It takes a little experience to learn how to control the heat and moisture inside your frame. Keep in mind these precautions when trying to grow out of season.

Extending Cool-Weather Crops into Summer

In addition to lettuce and radishes, you might also try growing spinach or even cabbage out of season into the early summer. Spring crops can be grown from seeds or from transplants started indoors a few weeks ahead of time. When choosing varieties of cool-weather crops to grow into summer, look for words like "long standing," "slow to bolt," and "heat resistant" in the seed catalogs or packet descriptions.

Summer

As the spring season progresses, it's time to give some summer vegetables—such as beans, squash, and cucumbers—a head start. For earlier harvests, try starting the seeds for these warm-weather crops right in their permanent location under a protective cage two weeks before the usual planting time. They will be much hardier and stronger than seedlings grown on the windowsill. When all danger of frost is past, remove the covers.

There is an entire industry with all kinds of protective devices and products to help the gardener be successful in early gardening. They vary from water-filled walls around the plant to special ground covers designed to heat up the soil quicker. Try some of these products and see what happens. I always like to place an unprotected plant right next to the protected one for comparison.

 SUMMER LETTUCE

Did you ever notice that just when all of the good summer salad vegetables are ready—like tomatoes, cucumbers, and peppers—the lettuce and radishes are all gone? In the hot, long days of summer, these spring crops bolt and set seed, becoming bitter and unappetizing. However, there is a way to get around this and still "have your salad and eat it, too!"

1. Cover lettuce with a shade cage (see Chapter 4 for instructions).
2. Give it twice as much as water as you normally would.
3. Cover the ground surrounding the lettuce with a thick layer of mulch.

Shade and Water

If you're the type of person who doesn't like hot, sticky weather, and you literally wilt in the sun, then the obvious solution is to move into the shade with a large pitcher of your favorite cold drink. Well, lettuce and radishes are no different. If you can provide shade for these spring crops (especially during the noon sun), along with some extra water, you will be able to harvest throughout most of the summer. Look for special hot-weather varieties of your favorite plants in your seed catalog.

Cover the square with a shade cage, and give the plants plenty of water—as a general rule, water twice as often as you usually would.

Remember, one of the best aids for growing a good crop is Mel's Mix—our soil mix that combines equal parts peat moss, coarse vermiculite, and blended compost. It holds lots of moisture so the plant roots can take up all that's needed, yet drains well so the roots can't become waterlogged.

MEL SAYS...

When all the summer crops grow in the same box it's easier to protect them from frost.

1. Cover summer crops with a PVC arch or wagon frame (see Chapter 4 for details).

2. Add a plastic cover and fasten down the corners, or

3. Cover the crops with loose hay.

Shade Screens

The shade cage will admit enough light for proper growth while keeping the temperature down considerably. A layer of thick mulch will also help moderate soil temperatures. You can also make use of natural shade or sun screens by locating a planting of spring crops behind (to the north of) your vertical growing frames.

Keep in mind that you're growing out of season, which means it is not the plant's natural inclination to grow then. You are urging these plants on, so be generous with your help and attention and don't expect too much. Just enjoy the challenge and experience!

Summer Plants into Fall

Gardeners sometimes wonder whether the extra effort involved in protecting summer crops from the first fall frost is worth the effort. I think it certainly is, if you want an extra two or three weeks worth of harvest from all those warm-weather crops. Quite often the first frost is followed by a long period of clear, warm weather before the next frost. If you can protect your garden from that first frost, you can enjoy green plants and fresh vegetables during one of the most pleasant periods of the year—mid-autumn. Since most of these crops have a six to eight week harvest season, the extra two to three weeks gained amount to quite a bit—more than a 25 percent extension of the season.

All Together Now

To protect your crops from frost, you can start with a PVC arch or covered wagon frame, and then cover it with a large sheet of plastic, floating cover, or light blanket. Fasten down the corners so it won't blow off during the night. Or, the low-growing crops can be readily protected with a loose covering of hay that is easily removed the next morning.

To protect vine crops from frost, just throw a blanket or tarp over the vertical frame so it's hanging down on all sides. This is one of the prime advantages of growing squash, tomatoes, cucumbers, pole beans, pumpkins, and similar summer crops on a vertical frame.

Fall

When fall arrives, you and your garden have three options: to store food for the winter, extend the harvest, or stop your garden. Whichever you choose depends on your time and desire.

Extending the Harvest by Storing It

Let's look at the easiest and least-known way to extend the harvest—storing it. There's the old-fashioned but economical canning, preserving, and freezing for the future, and it has a place. But I think the most economical and environmentally correct way to extend the season is to store the harvest. There is almost no work and money involved, and the flavor and nutritional value of each vegetable is greater than if it was frozen or canned.

Handle Your Harvest Gently

The only secret of successful storage is actually very simple—learn each vegetable's best storage conditions and provide it. There are really only two: cool and dry, or cold and moist. The list of vegetables that need cool and dry conditions is easy to remember because there are only a few—pumpkins, winter squash, and onions. The temperature should be around 50 to 60 degrees Fahrenheit (10 to 15.5 degrees Celsius), and the humidity needs to be fairly low—at about 50 percent.

MEL SAYS...

DON'T FEED THE ANIMALS
There is one problem with using hay bales as winter mulch—they can provide a cozy nest for ground mice and voles that love to eat crunchy root crops. If they do infest your winter storage plot, it's best to harvest everything and store your produce in a different place.

Try to find a cool corner of your garage or basement where the temperature stays above 35 but below 60 degrees F (above 1.6 but below 15.5 degrees C). If you think your storage area might freeze or get too warm at times, you can build two walls to enclose a corner to provide an even-temperature fruit closet. Add some insulation, and remember to allow plenty of air circulation. Don't stack produce up in a big pile, but spread your vegetables out evenly on a shelf (not on the floor).

Handle produce as gently and infrequently as possible. When you're out harvesting, treat each vegetable as if it were an egg. Any bruise or cut will be the first spot to spoil. Lay each harvested vegetable separately in a box of sawdust or crumpled newspaper; don't pile them all together. Do not wash or scrub the produce. Leave the bottom of the root on root crops, and at least an inch of the top growth. For crops such as vine crops, leave as much of the stem on as possible. Only store produce that is in really good condition.

Vegetables in the group that need cold and moist conditions are all root crops—beets, carrots, turnips, white potatoes, and winter radishes plus all of the cabbage family. This group also includes fruit—especially apples. The ideal storage temperature for them is as cold as you can get without actually freezing—35 to 45 degrees F (1.6 to 7.2 degrees C).

Actually, the simplest way to store root crops is not to dig them up at all. Roll a bale of hay over the planted area; this will break their tops and stop the plant's growing cycle while keeping the ground from freezing. When you're ready to harvest, simply roll the bale over, dig up a few vegetables, and then replace the bale. Regular radishes won't hold up too long in freezing weather while the winter radish will last almost indefinitely. Carrots and leeks also do quite well through the entire winter. If you're feeling adventurous, you can experiment with leaving different root crops in the ground to see which last through the fall and winter so you'll know what to expect the following year.

Cozy Cover

Cabbage and other leaf and head crops can also be stored in the garden, but they won't do well under a solid bale of hay. Instead, it is better to use a loose, fluffy covering of straw or leaves. To keep the wind from blowing this loose covering around, try placing a 2-foot-high fence of chicken wire around your garden areas and anchoring the wiring at each corner with stakes.

WRITE IT DOWN

Don't forget to draw a diagram of what's left in the garden and where so you won't be frantically digging around on a cold winter afternoon looking for the carrots but finding only radishes. The entire garden looks the same once the snow covers everything.

Dig It In

Another storage method for root crops is to bury a container in the ground and pack your vegetables in layers of moist sawdust, peat moss, or sand. You can sink a plastic or metal garbage can straight into the ground while keeping the top a few inches above the surface so no water gets in. Make sure the cover fits tightly; then pile at least 12 inches of hay or leaves over the top. Keep everything dry by covering it with a weighted-down plastic sheet or tarp. Watch out for leaks in the container that can allow groundwater to seep in. If you can, select an area on high ground to locate the storage container. The ground will not freeze under or around this container, and your vegetables will be maintained in a very even and moist condition.

Temperature Differences

On a cold night you can walk around your property and actually feel the differences in temperature. The cold air virtually rolls down the slope and settles in low-lying areas; in fact, this is called cold air drainage.

Surprisingly, this will happen even where there is not a great difference in elevation. Once you get the knack of watching out for frost and covering your plants when it threatens, you will see the advantages of locating a garden on the top or south side
of a slope rather than at the bottom of a low area. You will also see the advantage of grouping your crops according to their weather requirements. This makes it easier to protect them from either frost or freezing in both the spring and fall. One of the greatest advantages of SFG is how easy it is to protect your garden since it is condensed into small, uniform areas.

It's much simpler and more cost effective to grow cool-weather crops for an extended season using a sun-heated box that protects plants from just the severe weather fluctuations.

Frost

Frost forms when the outdoor temperature drops below the freezing point, resulting in the deposit of ice crystals. Plant material will freeze when there is an accumulation of cold air, 32 degrees Fahrenheit or below (0 degrees Celsius), at ground level. Frost can, and does, occur in low areas while the hills and slopes right next to them might be frost-free. This is because hot air rises and cold air sinks. If a body of water is nearby, it can greatly reduce the occurrence of frost as water holds heat very well.

In general, frost usually occurs in the very early morning hours, particularly after a still, calm night when the weather is dry. The chances of frost are also increased following the passage of a cold front, indicated by an intermittent and changing weather pattern of broken clouds and occasional precipitation; this is in contrast to the steady or continuous rain and the heavy, low-hanging clouds that accompany a warm front.

When frost is predicted, be ready. Your best bet is to catch the evening weather forecast, particularly the local one. Another (perhaps better) source is the Internet. One of the best websites is **www.weather.com.** Click on "Home and Garden," then "Lawn and Garden" and enter your zip code. You'll get all the information you need to be ready for that first frost.

Light Versus Hard Frost

A light frost blackens the outer leaves of most summer flowers and vegetables. It is indicated by a white covering on the lawn in very early morning. Summer vegetables can still be harvested if eaten right away.

A hard frost will blacken and kill all summer flowers and vegetables. Plants that were bushy and colorful the day before are now just droopy skeletons with blackened leaves hanging like rags from the stems. This can be very disheartening for gardeners who come out in the morning to find that the garden has been devastated. A hard frost is indicated by a crunchy feel to the ground and a thin film of ice on the birdbath. This is the time when most gardeners declare an end to the season. But if you have planted some colorful fall-blooming plants (mums, asters, and some hardy daisies) along with the fall vegetables, and you clean up the garden right away, your garden will still look attractive and inviting after a hard frost. Your spirits will be lifted and you can go on to enjoy an autumn garden.

Winter

Gardeners who are particularly ambitious and want to continue growing something all winter will need additional tools for providing special protection to a very select variety of plants. If you can keep the ground from freezing solid and provide sunlight in just a small area, in many parts of the country you can continue growing special varieties of lettuce and spinach, hardy leaf crops such as kale, and a number of oriental vegetables all winter long. It's also possible to plant some members of the onion family in the fall in order to get a larger or early crop next spring and summer. Call your county extension service for local advice and conditions.

GROWING WINTER VEGGIES

1. **Select fast-growing varieties with superior cold resistance.**
2. **Select the sunniest sheltered spot in your yard (it can be temporary).**
3. **Plant in a sheltered box.**

As you continue gardening, you'll learn which vegetables are hardier in your particular area. Wind and rain have a lot to do with plant survival and how much protection you need to provide.

Special Cold Varieties

Salad from your garden during the coldest months of winter? You bet. A fall box (that's just a SFG box that's used during the fall) can provide fresh salad each week during the winter without a greenhouse. Here's how: select fast-growing vegetables for your winter garden. Try any of the hardy salad greens and root crops, but look for special cold-tolerant varieties. Every seed company offers different varieties so look through catalogs and select those that are recommended for cold and winter growing. Look for names that have words in them like "Arctic," "Frost King," or "Snow Man" (I just made that last one up).

Pick a Spot

Now, pick the sunniest, most sheltered spot you can find for your winter garden. It doesn't have to be in the main garden; next to the house or garage is better, especially if you have white painted brick or stucco walls, since they will reflect quite a bit of heat into your miniature garden. Remember that the sun is very low in the sky during the winter, and the place that may have been in full sun during the summer could now very well be a very shady place in the winter. Don't place the box under the roof or gutter line, or you'll risk the chance that rain, sleet, or snow will fall on it. You'll be in good shape if the area is sheltered from strong winter winds and if it gets a maximum amount of winter sunlight. It doesn't have to be a permanent spot either. First, lay down a sheet of plastic or sturdy weed cloth and in the spring you can pick everything up and return the area back to its former use.

Snuggle Up

Install your winter box, fill it with Mel's Mix, and start your planting. Since the plants will grow very slowly compared to spring and summer and since you'll be harvesting every leaf almost as it is ready, you can plant your produce closer than the usual spacing, even as close as one-half the recommended distance.

Insulate

Provide some insulation around the winter box, by banking the outside with soil or placing bales of hay all around. Provide a tight-fitting cover or make a double-layer cover with plastic to keep the soil and air from losing heat at night. Throw a blanket or tarp on the box for those extra cold nights.

Putting Your Garden to Bed

When it is time to put the SFG to bed, we do this the same way we put our children to bed. You wouldn't think of sending them to their room and paying no attention to them would you? Instead, we encourage them to prepare for bedtime—to brush their teeth, get one last drink, fix the bed just the way they want it, and then spend some time reading a bedtime story. Then it's finally lights out.

Well, treat your garden the same way. Don't leave it a mess with dead plants and debris lying about. Tidy it up and make it look good. Now is an excellent time to mix a little extra compost in each box and smooth and level it out so it will be all ready for the spring planting. That's never happened before with single-row gardening. Now it's not only possible, but also very practical.

The little extra work you do in the fall will keep your garden attractive and neat-looking all winter and make your springtime garden easier to begin. You'll simply go out, rake off the mulch cover (remember your rototilling neighbor?), and start planting either at the regular time or early.

Grids in Winter

You can remove, clean, fold, and hang up the grids now or leave them on the boxes all winter, which will remind you of how much fun you have now with gardening. What I'm suggesting for the end of the season is really no different than what I recommend you do all season long. Keep your garden neat, tidy, and attractive. If you keep it in tip-top condition (and that's not too difficult with a no-work garden), you will enjoy it so much more.

Take Notes

The only thing you might want to do is record in a notebook or journal some of the highlights of this past year—notes for improvements, special varieties of plants, and tips for next year.

Decorate for the Holidays

You'll enjoy SFG much more if you keep your garden neat and attractive at all times. Since you no longer have to hoe the weeds or dig and cultivate the soil, you'll have time and energy for the pleasant things like trimming off yellow or dead lower leaves, dead blossoms, removing plants, or dead and pest-damaged leaves or entire plants.

But what about winter? Not much work to do after putting the garden to bed, but you might think about decorating the garden so it still looks nice all winter long or at least for the holidays.

Thanksgiving

Make a nice arrangement in one or more boxes of a fall scene, like a stack of corn with pumpkins. Some of the boxes could just have a bale or two of hay or straw. Maybe even a scarecrow in a box. Those boxes could be covered with cloth (like white garden floating covers) or old colored sheets tacked or stapled down.

Christmas or Winter

Here are some ideas that will make your SFG festive during the bleak winter months.

1. Make Christmas boxes out of your garden boxes by using old colored or striped sheets, a tarp or table cloth, or floating garden covers.

2. Think ahead when you go to yard sales or the thrift shop. Many covers could serve double duty as frost covers in the fall, then decorative covers in the winter.

3. Use wide, colorful ribbon, rope, or contrasting colored strips of sheets to tie bows on the boxes. Tuck in greens and pine cones, even lights if you can get an extension cord to the garden. (Remember now, your garden no longer needs to be way out back; it can be right near your back door where you'll see it more often.)

4. Decorate your vertical frames with decorative lights, pine branches, pine cones, and bird feeders.

After Christmas, stick a discarded Christmas tree in the center of each box, and make them into bird feeders, with or without lights. Tie a string from each box corner to the treetop for support.

Start Small

This chapter teaches us how to extend all the seasons and how doing that can give us an extra 50 percent of gardening time. How exciting! If you read through all this and felt a little discouraged or glazed-over, don't worry. If you have never grown out-of-season, add just a few features here and there as you gain more confidence. It can be a really fun challenge to any gardener—regardless of experience. As with all new gardening projects, my recommendation is to start small in order to gain experience, confidence, and pleasure—then expand. And just in case you need more convincing, remember that All New Square Foot Gardening eliminates so many gardening tasks so you have the time and energy to extend the seasons.

OUT WITH THE OLD

OLD WAY	NEW WAY
1. Clean off summer residue	Do this daily and it won't accumulate
2. Turn over the soil	No longer necessary
3. Perform a pH test	No longer necessary
4. Add all the humus you can get	No longer necessary
5. Add peat moss if no humus	No longer necessary
6. Add new 3 to 6 inch layer	No longer necessary
7. Dig in manure or leaf mold	No longer necessary
8. Add some fertilizer	No longer necessary
9. Use a fork, shovel, spade	No longer necessary—use trowel
10. Dig as deep as you can	No longer necessary
11. Deeper is better	No longer necessary
12. Break up clods, remove stones	No longer necessary

Mel's Final Summary

Well—there you have it! The ALL NEW Square Foot Gardening System with the latest updates and improvements I've made to the original system I invented thirty years ago.

In closing, I'd like to highlight the most important features of SFG for you so you truly understand why it's so different from the old-fashioned, outdated single-row gardening system we've all been taught at one time or another. Square Foot Gardening is sort of like a picture puzzle of an attractive garden ready for harvest—and there's only sixteen large pieces to fit together to produce the finished picture (that is, the harvest). To produce the same harvest-picture, the single-row garden has 489 tiny pieces to fit together!

The features of SFG will help you understand how one thing relates to another and how all the simplifications of SFG fit together to help each other produce a much better garden for you—without a lot of work and knowledge. Here are the most important and far reaching of those features.

Location

Since Square Foot Gardening takes only 20 percent of the space to produce 100 percent of the harvest, it can be located almost anywhere—and the best location is close to the house. That's where you'll pass it more often, notice and appreciate it more and as a result, you'll take better care of it. This will produce a better and more productive garden.

Size

The same thing applies to protecting your garden from just about anything harmful, weather and pests being the most destructive; the smaller size makes everything easier to maintain and control. Size also applies to who can garden; this manageable size means everyone—even those with limited time or energy—can enjoy the benefits of the garden.

Soil Requirements

We've eliminated all the things you used to have to learn about soil and the special requirements for each individual vegetable—because now you're using nothing but Mel's Mix. If you make yours according to the formula and if you use a good blended compost made from at least five ingredients, you'll have a perfect soil for every single crop in your garden. We won't have to tell you to screen for stones, or add extra humus, or that this crop needs a higher pH or a well-drained soil . . . or any of those things that most books have to tell you. You're starting out with a perfect soil for every single crop. So we don't have to give you different or special directions about soil for every single plant.

Location for Sunlight

All the vegetables need lots of sun: six to eight hours per day. If any of your garden area gets more sun than other areas, that's the place to put your warm weather or summer crops. The spring and fall cool weather crops can get by with less sun, and in fact will do better in the summer if they do not have as much sun as the other summer crops. Of course, if your entire garden gets the same amount of sunlight, plant cool weather crops in the partial shade of a taller plant—or provide them with one of the simple sun shades described in Chapter 4.

Fertilizer

We don't use fertilizer anymore. We don't need it. Mel's Mix—with its rich compost—has all the natural nutrients, trace elements, and minerals that any of the plants could possibly want. You won't need to learn that this plant needs extra nitrogen or that plant needs extra potassium—because Mel's Mix has everything each plant needs, and it is readily available for them. Those that need it, take it. Those that don't need it, don't take it. It's that simple; it's that easy. You won't have to learn anything about fertilizer or the various formulas or what NPK means . . . you won't have to go to the store to buy fertilizer at all. Think of the time and money you'll save! The best part—it's all natural and organic. Is that easy gardening or what?

But besides all that, you're going to have a perfect garden because you're starting with a perfect soil. I'm sure you are tired of hearing about it, but the value and importance of the proper soil mix cannot be overemphasized. After you become successful with your garden and begin helping others start their new SFG, please be as emphatic as I am about the proper soil mix. It virgually guarantees success.

Watering

The same goes for watering. The general directions for watering in the Square Foot Garden are to make sure the soil stays moist, and give the plants as much water as they need. Although that sounds nebulous at first, you will soon become acclimated to those directions, and you'll know which plants require more. (Of course, it all depends on size, season, weather, and the growth pattern of that particular plant.) Anyone can see that a large bushy plant needs much more than a young seedling just starting. No matter what method of watering you use, another important feature of Mel's Mix is that you or your sprinkler system can't overwater, because this mix drains out all the excess water.

Pests and Diseases

We also won't go into any detail of possible pests and diseases of each individual plant. I've had gardeners tell me that when they read a long list of potential threats, they often decide they don't want to grow that crop—and that's a shame, because in all likelihood, they'll never see that pest or disease.

I think you have seen by now that SFG is not about all the problems and diseases of plant growth, it is about healthy productive plants growing in a garden starting with healthy natural soil. As we explained in an earlier chapter, if you have a problem or some pests (if you can first identify or describe it), call your local county extension agent and describe it. They can not only tell you what it is, but how to get rid of it. In addition, they know your expected frost dates and the best varieties to grow in your local area.

Our feeling, of course, is that with your natural rich soil, you won't have most problems; the plants will grow healthy and they'll be much more resistant to any disease or pest.

When to Plant

Charts in the following pages will give you all of the information you need to know about when to plant both seeds or seedlings, indoors or out. They also indicate when to replant an additional crop in order to have a continuous harvest through the gardening year.

Planting Charts

GERMINATION TIMES AND TEMPERATURES

This chart shows the number of days required for vegetable seeds to sprout at different temperatures.

CROP	32°F	41°F	50°F	59°F	68°F	77°F	86°F	95°F
Beans	0	0	0	16	11	8	6	6
Beets	–	42	17	10	6	5	5	5
Cabbage	–	–	15	9	6	5	4	–
Carrots	0	51	17	10	7	6	6	9
Cauliflower	–	–	20	10	6	5	5	–
Corn	0	0	22	12	7	4	4	3
Cucumbers	0	0	0	13	6	4	3	3
Eggplant	–	–	–	–	13	8	5	–
Lettuce	49	15	7	4	3	2	3	0
Muskmelons	–	–	–	–	8	4	3	–
Onions	136	31	13	7	5	4	4	13
Parsley	–	–	29	17	14	13	12	–
Peas	–	36	14	9	8	6	6	–
Peppers	0	0	0	25	13	8	6	9
Radishes	0	29	11	6	4	4	3	–
Spinach	63	23	12	7	6	5	6	0
Tomatoes	0	0	43	14	8	6	6	9

0 = Little or no germination   — = Not tested

Adapted from J. F. Harrington Agricultural Extension Leaflet, 1954.

OUTDOOR PLANTING SCHEDULE FOR SPRING AND SUMMER CROPS

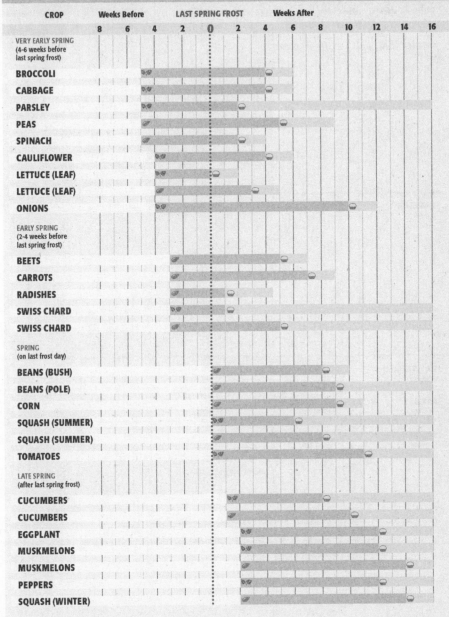

CROP	Weeks Before	LAST SPRING FROST	Weeks After

VERY EARLY SPRING
(4-6 weeks before
last spring frost)

BROCCOLI
CABBAGE
PARSLEY
PEAS
SPINACH
CAULIFLOWER
LETTUCE (LEAF)
LETTUCE (LEAF)
ONIONS

EARLY SPRING
(2-4 weeks before
last spring frost)

BEETS
CARROTS
RADISHES
SWISS CHARD
SWISS CHARD

SPRING
(on last frost day)

BEANS (BUSH)
BEANS (POLE)
CORN
SQUASH (SUMMER)
SQUASH (SUMMER)
TOMATOES

LATE SPRING
(after last spring frost)

CUCUMBERS
CUCUMBERS
EGGPLANT
MUSKMELONS
MUSKMELONS
PEPPERS
SQUASH (WINTER)

LEGEND: = Growth Period, started with seeds   = Growth Period, started with transplants   = Harvest Period

PLANTING SCHEDULE FOR CONTINUOUS HARVEST CROPS

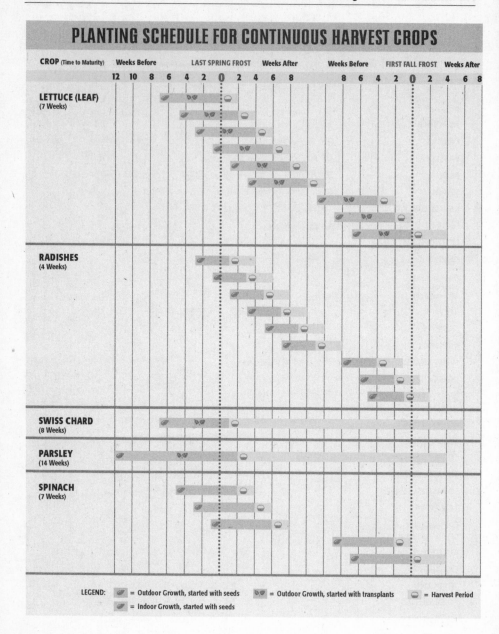

LEGEND: = Outdoor Growth, started with seeds   = Outdoor Growth, started with transplants   = Harvest Period

  = Indoor Growth, started with seeds

PLANTING SCHEDULE FOR CONTINUOUS HARVEST CROPS

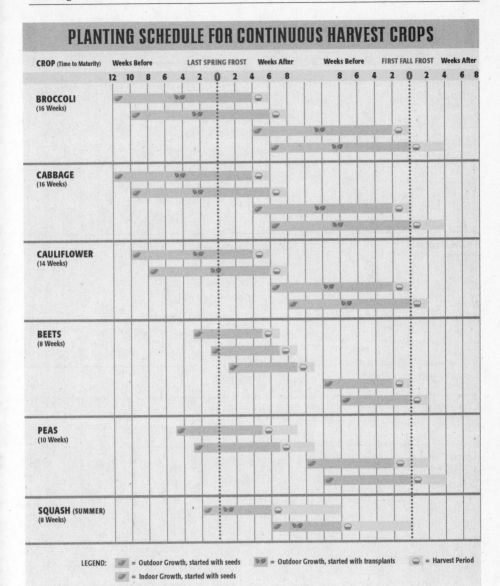

LEGEND: = Outdoor Growth, started with seeds   = Outdoor Growth, started with transplants   = Harvest Period

= Indoor Growth, started with seeds

PLANTING SCHEDULE FOR CONTINUOUS HARVEST CROPS

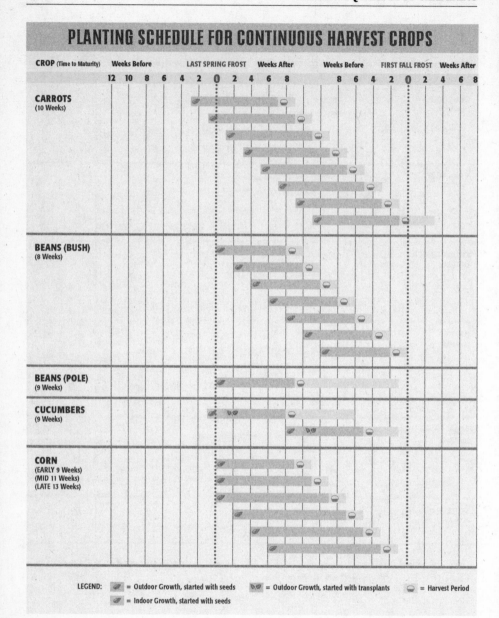

LEGEND: = Outdoor Growth, started with seeds   = Outdoor Growth, started with transplants   = Harvest Period
= Indoor Growth, started with seeds

PLANTING SCHEDULE FOR CONTINUOUS HARVEST CROPS

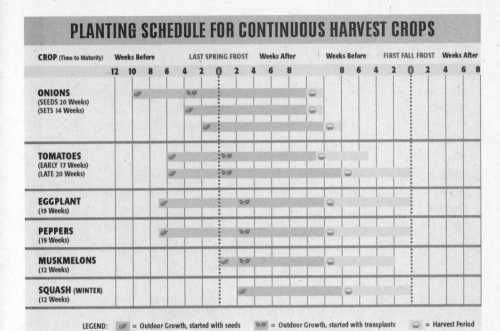

LEGEND: = Outdoor Growth, started with seeds   = Outdoor Growth, started with transplants   = Harvest Period

= Indoor Growth, started with seeds

PLANTING SCHEDULE FOR FALL CROPS

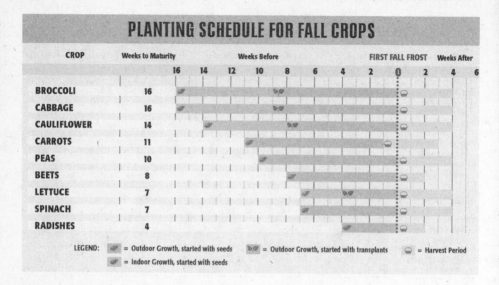

CROP	Weeks to Maturity	Weeks Before							FIRST FALL FROST		Weeks After	
		16	14	12	10	8	6	4	2	0	2	4	6
BROCCOLI	16												
CABBAGE	16												
CAULIFLOWER	14												
CARROTS	11												
PEAS	10												
BEETS	8												
LETTUCE	7												
SPINACH	7												
RADISHES	4												

LEGEND: = Outdoor Growth, started with seeds = Outdoor Growth, started with transplants = Harvest Period = Indoor Growth, started with seeds

CROPS FOR A FALL HARVEST

SUMMER CROPS STILL GROWING (HARVEST CONTINUES UNTIL FIRST FROST)	NEW OUTDOOR PLANTINGS IN MIDSUMMER (5–10 WEEKS BEFORE FIRST FALL FROST)	NEW OUTDOOR PLANTINGS IN LATE SUMMER (0–5 WEEKS BEFORE FIRST FALL FROST)
Beans	Broccoli	Lettuce
Swiss Chard	Cabbage	Radishes
Corn	Cauliflower	
Cucumber	Beets	
Eggplant	Carrots	
Peppers	Lettuce	
Muskmelon	Spinach	
Winter Squash	Peas	
Tomatoes		

LEGEND: = Plant Seeds = Plant Transplants

AT A GLANCE

VEGETABLES

Name	Family	Height	Spacing per square foot	Growing season	Weeks from seed to harvest	Years you can store seeds
Asparagus	Lily	4-6 feet	1 or 4	spring, summer	3 years	3
Bean, Bush	Pulse	12-18 inches	9	summer	8	3-4
Bean, Pole	Pulse	4-7 feet	8	summer	10	3-4
Beet	Goosefoot	12 inches	large - 9 small - 16	spring, summer, fall	8	4-5
Broccoli	Mustard	18-24 inches	1	spring, fall	16	5-6
Cabbage	Mustard	12-18 inches	1	spring, fall	16	5-6
Carrot	Carrot	12 inches	16	spring, summer, fall, winter*	10	3-4
Cauliflower	Mustard	18-24 inches	1	spring, fall	14	5-6
Chard, Swiss	Goosefoot	12-18 inches	4	spring, summer, fall, winter*	8	4-5
Corn	Grass	5-6 feet	4	summer	9-13	1-2
Cucumber	Gourd	vine	2	summer	9	5-6
Eggplant	Nightshade	24-30 inches	1	summer	19	5-6
Lettuce	Composite	6-12 inches	4	spring, summer*, fall, winter*	7	5-6
Melon	Gourd	vine	1 per 2 sq. ft.	summer	12	5-6
Okra	Lily	18-24 inches	1	summer	12	2
Onion	Lily	12 inches	16	spring, summer	20	1-2
Parsley	Carrot	6-12 inches	4	spring, summer, fall, winter*	14	2-3
Pea, Sugar Snap	Pulse	vine	8	spring, fall	10	3-4
Pepper	Nightshade	12-24 inches	1	summer	19	4-5
Potato	Nightshade	12-24 inches	4	spring, summer, fall	12	Plant last year's potatoes
Radish	Mustard	6-12 inches	16	spring, summer*, fall	4	5-6
Spinach	Goosefoot	6-12 inches	9	spring, fall, winter*	7	5-6
Strawberry	Rose	6-12 inches	4	spring, fall	perennial	Use plants
Summer Squash	Gourd	bush vine	1 per 9 sq. ft. 1 per 2 sq. ft.	summer	8	5-6
Winter Squash	Gourd	vine	1 per 2 sq. ft.	summer	12	5-6
Tomato	Nightshade	bush vine	1 per 9 sq. ft. 1 per 1 sq. ft.	summer	17	4-5

AT A GLANCE

HERBS

Name	Family	Height	Spacing per square foot	Growing season	Weeks from seed to harvest	Years you can store seeds
Basil	Mint	1-2 feet	small-4 large-1	summer	12	5
Chive	Lily	6-12 inches	16	late spring, summer	16	2
Cilantro	Umbellifer	1-2 feet	1	late spring, summer	5 (leaves) 12 (seeds)	N/A
Mint	Mint	1-3 feet	1	spring, summer, fall	N/A	N/A
Oregano	Mint	1-2 feet	1	spring, summer, fall	16	N/A

AT A GLANCE

FLOWERS

Name	Family	Height	Spacing per square foot	Growing season	Weeks from seed to harvest	Years you can store seeds
Dahlia	Daisy	1-3 feet	small-4 medium-1	summer, fall	10-12	2-3
Dusty Miller	Daisy	12-18 inches	4	late spring, summer, fall	15	N/A
Marigold	Daisy	6-12 inches 1 1/2-3 feet	dwarf-4, large-1	summer, fall	10	2-3
Pansy	Viola	6-9 inches	4	spring, summer (if cool), fall	20	N/A
Petunia	Nightshade	6-18 inches	4	late spring, summer, early fall	14	N/A
Salvia	Mint	1-2 feet	4	late spring, summer, early fall	14	1 (use fresh seed)

*In some parts of the country and under certain weather conditions, these can be grown in this season.

N/A = Not advised to store seed.

Meet Mel Bartholomew

Mel Bartholomew's path to arguably the most influential backyard gardener was an untraditional one. A civil engineer by profession and frustrated gardener by weekend, Bartholomew was convinced unmanageable single-row gardening was a waste of energy and output. After his research yielded responses such as "but that's the way we've always done it," Bartholomew condensed the unmanageable single-row space to 4×4 feet, amended the soil, and bingo… he developed a gardening system that yields 100% of the harvest in 20% of the space.

Bartholomew's Square Foot Method quickly gained popularity and strength, ultimately converting more than one million gardeners worldwide. "Square Foot Gardening," the highest-rated PBS gardening show to date, launched in 1981 and ran weekly for five years, followed later by a weekly Square Foot Show on the Discovery Network. In 1986 the creation of the Square Foot Gardening Foundation and the "A Square Yard in the School Yard Program" brought the technique to an estimated 3,000 schools nationwide.

As fan mail and testimonials from thousands of gardeners across the country arrived, Bartholomew realized that his Square Foot Method was relevant on a global scale. Converted into Square Meter Gardening, Bartholomew seized an opportunity to bring the dietary benefits of his revolutionary system to millions of malnourished Third World citizens. His global humanitarian effort, orchestrated through the Square Meter International Training Centers in Lehigh, Utah and Homestead, Florida, trained international humanitarian organizations and leaders in the Square Meter Method. Since its launch, Bartholomew's global outreach initiative has spread from Africa to Asia to South America and is recognized as a resounding success by nonprofit human interest groups.

And there are no signs of slowing down. Bartholomew's global outreach continues throughout the world while closer to home, attention has shifted to increasing the Square Foot presence in the California school system. Bartholomew is determined to continue and strengthen the well established Square Foot programs and institutions across the nation and the globe.

Bartholomew operates his nonprofit Square Foot Gardening foundation in Eden, Utah.